Hay West

A Story of Canadians Helping Canadians

Hay West

A STORY OF CANADIANS HELPING CANADIANS

Bob Plamondon

Red Deer PRESS

PUBLISHED BY
Red Deer Press
813 MacKimmie Library Tower
2500 University Drive N.W.
Calgary Alberta Canada T2N 1N4
www.reddeerpress.com

CREDITS
Edited for the Press by Dennis Johnson
Cover and text design by Erin Woodward
Cover images courtesy Hay West volunteers. Hay field image courtesy Corel. Back cover image courtesy the Ottawa Citizen. Picture of children courtesy the Wainwright Review.
Printed and bound in Canada by Friesens for Red Deer Press

ACKNOWLEDGMENTS
Financial support provided by the Canada Council, the Government of Canada through the Book Publishing Industry Development Program (BPIDP), the Alberta Foundation for the Arts, a beneficiary of the Lottery Fund of the Government of Alberta, and the University of Calgary.

NATIONAL LIBRARY OF CANADA CATALOGUING IN PUBLICATION
Plamondon, Robert E.
Hay West : a story of Canadians helping Canadians / Bob Plamondon.
ISBN 0-88995-315-5
1. Hay West Initiative. 2. Droughts—Prairie Provinces.
3. Farmers—Canada. 4. Voluntarism—Canada. I. Title.
FC3244.9.D76P53 2004   971.07′1   C2004-905667-0

Contents

HAY WEST DEDICATION

This book is dedicated to the enduring spirit of the Canadian farmer.

HAY WEST ACKNOWLEDGEMENT

Hay West gratefully acknowledges seed funding provided by Agriculture and Agri-Food Canada to assist in the preparation of this book.

AUTHOR'S DEDICATION

This book is dedicated to the sparkling lights in my life: my mother Jeannette Plamondon, my children Nathaniel and Charlotte; my loving wife Marian; and our child Megan Alexandra.

AUTHOR'S ACKNOWLEDGEMENT

I am grateful to those who helped in the research and writing of this book. Those who read various manuscripts and offered considerable guidance include June Coke, Cheryl McWilliams, Kurt Rufelds and Patty Townsend. I am fortunate to have found Red Deer Press, whose publisher, Dennis Johnson, brought a family background in farming and a mastery of the publishing business to this project. Ian Hamilton, our publishing consultant, gave his considerable energy, creativity and tenacity to ensure this book was published and widely distributed. Finally, I am most grateful to Phil McNeely and the entire Hay West Board of Directors for the opportunity to participate in this wonderful national initiative.

It gives me great pleasure to provide introductory remarks for this book recounting the 2002 Hay West Initiative.

In the summer of 2002, agricultural producers in drought-stricken regions of Alberta and Saskatchewan were faced with a severe shortage of feed. In Central and Eastern Canada, farmers were blessed with a surplus of quality hay. The Hay West Initiative was created in an effort to share these resources, and the Governments of Canada and Alberta, as well as corporate and private sponsors, contributed on a number of fronts to help with the overall hay delivery and collection effort. Between July and November, more then 1,000 producers donated over 60,000 large bales of hay to affected areas of Western Canada.

This book presents a wonderful opportunity to celebrate the tremendous generosity of countless volunteers, donors and sponsors who worked so hard and selflessly on behalf of their fellow Canadians. Indeed, Hay West has served as an outstanding illustration of the strength and generosity of the human spirit, and is a noble continuation of the great Canadian tradition of sharing and caring.

Please accept my best wishes.

Jean Chrétien

Ottawa 2003

If there is one thing farmers can deal with, especially in Alberta, it is weather. However when the weather they experience is the worst drought in 133 years of recorded history, they need a little more than support: they need hope.

Hay West provided them with that hope, by showing that Canadians from across the country were not only willing to donate their hay and money, but also their time and resources to get those much-needed hay supplies to Alberta producers. Funding was provided to Alberta's 4-H organization to assist the various 4-H clubs throughout rural Alberta in securing hay supplies for their local projects.

Numerous fundraising events were held throughout Alberta, and the Alberta Government provided $250,000 to help cover the cost of shipping the hay to Alberta. But most notable were the two "Hay West" concerts in Edmonton and Calgary. It was very heartening to see the musicians volunteer their services for the benefit of Alberta producers. As I did at the time, I would like to extend my thanks to everyone involved in the Hay West organization across Canada, including volunteers from across Canada who helped with the challenging task of moving that much hay that far; you have truly shown us what it means to be a Canadian.

October 2003

On behalf of the Government of Saskatcewan, I would like to take this opportunity to again thank our fellow Canadians from Eastern Canada for their generosity during the devastating drought of 2002.

That year marked the second year of an extensive drought in many areas of Saskatchewan and Western Canada. Because of the dry conditions, some areas of our province experienced a severe drop in hay prodcution, leaving many livestock prodcuers without adequate winter feed sources. In response, numerous people in eastern Canada took part in an attempt to get donated feed supplies into the hands of drought-stricken Prairie livestock producers.

The Hay West Campaign not only provided much needed feed for Prairie cattle, it became a national rallying point and showed Prairie producers they would not have to go through this struggle alone. I strongly believe the underlying message of the Hay West Campaign was to reinforce the fact that Canadians care about each other. When crisis occurs in one region of the country, other regions are there to lend a hand.

Undoubtedly, the past several years have been difficult for everyone involved in the agricultal industry. This important sector of our economy has faced major challenges which have put significant stress on rural communities and farm families. In spite of these difficulties, the foundation of our industry remains strong. Saskatchewan producers have been through difficult periods before, but our farmers and communities are resilient and have overcome these challenges. It is extremely comforting to know that this industry is valued by all Canadians, as proven by the 2002 Hay West Campaign. The generosity and kindness of everyone involved in this endeavour will not be forgotten.

Lorne Calvert
Premier

Preface

Hay West is a heart-warming story. It is about farmers helping farmers, neighbors helping neighbors, the East supporting the West and the goodwill and generosity of Canadians. It is also about two modest farmers from Navan, Ontario, who made a difference in ways that would have been hard to imagine.

Hay West began one early July morning at the farmhouse of Willard McWilliams when he saw a television on *Canada AM* about the drastic plight of Western farmers suffering from the worst recorded drought in over 133 years. Farmers had no feed for their animals, and many were being forced to sell their cattle. Some were at risk of losing their farms.

Willard and his son Wyatt were in the hay business. That summer it was clear to the McWilliams and other farmers throughout Eastern Canada that they were going to enjoy a hay crop of abundant proportions—more than what local farmers would need.

The McWilliams were also leaders in their communities and in farming organizations. Of note, a few years earlier they had been cited in the *Guinness Book of World Records* for driving a 50-horse hitch. They are men of big dreams. They knew that July morning that they had to find a way to help fellow farmers in need.

Only four months after watching that news telecast, the McWilliams had spearheaded a relief effort that delivered about 60,000 large bales of high-quality donated hay to

An Ontario farm, where the 2002 crop of hay was abundant.
Photo: Corel.

farmers in Saskatchewan and Alberta. They gave the farmers much more than hay: they gave them hope.

This Hay West story is about how this national relief effort got off the ground; how farmers spanning some 4,000 kilometers were mobilized; how the logistics of shipping and tracking 30,000 tonnes of hay were developed; how the story captured the hearts of many thousands of Canadians through the media; how some things went right and some went wrong; and how Hay West has become an important part of Canadian history in what it teaches about grassroots mobilization of disaster relief.

But the most compelling part of the Hay West story is how a few small-scale farmers with big hearts and big dreams captured the attention of a nation and gave hope to those in despair. If something like Hay West can happen, it makes you think that anything is possible.

This book is based on the personal accounts of those involved, thousands of media reports, extracts from *Hansard,* numerous Internet references and the many documents maintained and retained by Hay West. Any quote used in the book not otherwise footnoted was taken from a personal interview with the author. Extensive interviews were conducted with Hay West founders and its general manger over a two-year period. Most of the other interviews from which quotes were drawn were conducted in the fall of 2002. These included the following: Hon. Don Boudria, Government House Leader (November 17 and December 7) Hon. Lyle Vanclief, Minister of Agriculture (November 18); Kevin Sorenson MP (September 18); Carol Skelton MP (October 30); Myron Thompson MP (December 7); Marjory Loveys, Office of the Prime Minister (November 10); Randy Fletcher, Office of the Minister of Agriculture (November 18) Bruce Banks, Alberta 4-H (November 3); Pierre Corriveau and Jim McKendy, Agriculture and Agri-Food Canada (November 20); Marcel Dawson and Steve Palisek, Canadian Food Inspection Agency (October 29); Jim Feeney, CN Rail (November 13); Nikky Smith, Saskatchewan Cattle Feeders Association (December 8); Dave Cameron and Cathy Willoughby, Hay West staff (November 5); Doug Woodburn and Lloyd Craig, Hay West board of directors (December 8); and James Allen, Ottawa Central Railroad (January 6, 2004). The book is also enhanced by numerous photographs taken mostly by members of the McWilliams' family and other Hay West volunteers.

Every dollar contributed by Canadians to the Hay West Initiative was used to bring donated hay to farmers in need in Alberta and Saskatchewan. Hay West still exists, ready to assist Canadian farmers in the future. All net royalties from the sale of this book will be used by Hay West to help farmers in need.

Drought in Western Canada

Farmers know how to complain about the weather. They are famous for it. In 2002, however, farmers from eastern Canada needed to find something else to complain about. Growing conditions were so spectacular that many producers were leaving a potential third cut of hay in the fields because the first two harvests were early and bountiful. The haying season in the East, which normally runs into September, was in the barn by early August.

The chart on the page following shows that throughout 2002, rainfall in the Ottawa area exceeded normal levels, particularly at the beginning of the year when it does crops the most good.

Conditions in Western Canada could not have been more different. In fact, the dry conditions in 2002 were reported to be worse than those of the 1930s.[1] Indeed, the drought of 2002 earned Environment Canada's award for the top news story of the year—for bad news, that is. If it were not for modern no-till conservation farming practices, the affected areas of the West might well have been reminiscent of the Depression, when storms of dust known as Black Blizzards blew topsoil a thousand feet into the air.

Perhaps one drought year, even a horrific year, wouldn't be so bad if the years preceding had experienced normal rainfalls. But Western lands entered the 2002 growing season with a water deficit, the result of five successive years of lower-than-normal levels of precipitation. The low soil moisture reserves resulted in delayed seeding, poor crop germination and late plant development. For crops to ger-

The low water level of Fleeing Horse Lake near Provost, Alberta, demonstrates the extent of the drought to hit Western Canada in 2002. In the background, to the left stands the Provost Seed Cleaning Plant and to the right, the Agricore-United elevator awaiting delivery of a harvest that would never arrive.
Photo: Richard Holmes, *The Provost News*.

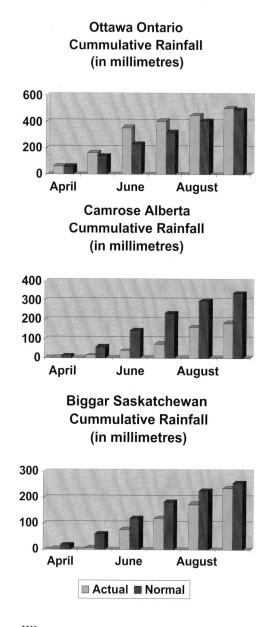

**Ottawa Ontario
Cummulative Rainfall
(in millimetres)**

**Camrose Alberta
Cummulative Rainfall
(in millimetres)**

**Biggar Saskatchewan
Cummulative Rainfall
(in millimetres)**

■ Actual ■ Normal

All charts courtesy of Environment Canada.

minate properly, farmers needed a rainfall that exceeded the annual average by 60 percent. Instead, the rainfall in 2002 fell short of the average by 60 percent. Not seen since the weatherman began recording annual weather conditions had a growing season been so poor.

The chart opposite depicts the actual and normal cumulative rainfall for April to September 2002 in millimeters for one of the affected areas, Camrose Alberta. In a normal year, the region would receive 145.5 mm of rainfall during the period. By the end of June, however, only 38.5 mm of rain, 26.5 percent of average, had fallen.

The situation in Biggar, Saskatchewan, was a little better, but the extremely low level of precipitation in April and May made seeding very difficult. If a seed doesn't sprout, it goes dormant. By the end of that critical early growing period in June, Biggar had received only 61.8 percent of normal levels.

Those following the 2002 drought may have been confused at times by apparently conflicting reports because conditions varied greatly across the West. The following map prepared by the Prairie Farm Rehabilitation Administration illustrates the variability of the 2002 drought. It reveals that most of central and northern Alberta faced extremely low rainfall or record dry conditions, while the pockets of drought in Saskatchewan were less prominent. Areas hardest hit stretched across central Alberta and into eastern Saskatchewan. However, areas in the deep south of Alberta and Saskatchewan experienced abnormally high rainfall.

Heat was also an issue in the West for 2002. What was dry was also hot, as can be seen on the Prairie Farm Rehabilitation Administration map, which appears on page 22, depicting the higher-than-average temperatures for all of central and northern Alberta and Saskatchewan.

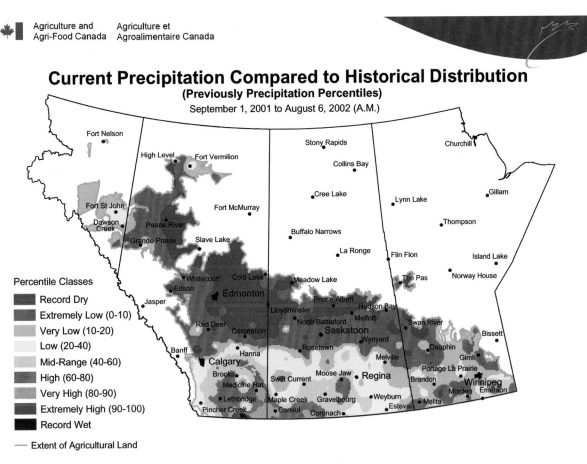

Agriculture and
Agri-Food Canada

Agriculture et
Agroalimentaire Canada

Current Precipitation Compared to Historical Distribution
(Previously Precipitation Percentiles)
September 1, 2001 to August 6, 2002 (A.M.)

Percentile Classes

- Record Dry
- Extremely Low (0-10)
- Very Low (10-20)
- Low (20-40)
- Mid-Range (40-60)
- High (60-80)
- Very High (80-90)
- Extremely High (90-100)
- Record Wet
- — Extent of Agricultural Land

Prepared by PFRA (Prairie Farm Rehabilitation Administration) using data from the Timely Climate Monitoring Network and the many federal and provincial agencies and volunteers that support it.

All maps courtesy Prairie Farm Rehabilitation Administration.

Canada

The deadly combination of no moisture and high temperatures sealed the fate of the 2002 growing season. When rain finally came, it was a deluge that washed away parched fields and left the meager crops unharvestable. When it wasn't unbearably hot, the weather cooled to record levels, which included the earliest August frost in 109 years.[2] The result was poor to negligible grass growth in all but the most southern parts of Alberta and Saskatchewan.

Statistics Canada reported: "The 2002 crop year will be remembered as one of the worst growing seasons for Western

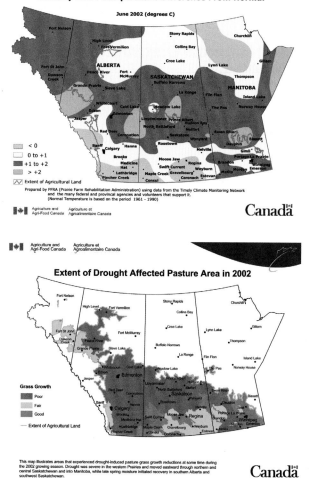

Monthly Mean Temperature Difference From Normal

June 2002 (degrees C)

- [light] < 0
- [white] 0 to +1
- [dark] +1 to +2
- [grey] > +2
- Extent of Agricultural Land

Prepared by PFRA (Prairie Farm Rehabilitation Administration) using data from the Timely Climate Monitoring Network and the many federal and provincial agencies and volunteers that support it.
(Normal Temperature is based on the period 1961 - 1990)

Agriculture and Agri-Food Canada   Agriculture et Agroalimentaire Canada

Canada

Agriculture and Agri-Food Canada   Agriculture et Agroalimentaire Canada

Extent of Drought Affected Pasture Area in 2002

Grass Growth
- Poor
- Fair
- Good

Extent of Agricultural Land

This map illustrates areas that experienced drought-induced pasture grass growth reductions at some time during the 2002 growing season. Drought was severe in the western Prairies and moved eastward through northern and central Saskatchewan and into Manitoba, while late spring moisture initiated recovery in southern Alberta and southwest Saskatchewan.

Canada

Grazing land near St. Paul, Alberta, was typically a verdant green in late spring, but in 2002 it was brown and parched.
Photo: Terry Siemers *The LakeLander.*

Canada. Hardest hit are producers in Alberta, where the spring wheat crop is expected to decline 50% from 2001; barley production will be down 44% and canola, 57%."[3] The crop failure in Western Canada was so profound that the Canadian Wheat Board dropped out of world markets because there was not enough wheat to sell to new customers.

While Environment Canada data can statistically portray the severity of the 2002 drought, Crowfoot Alberta Member of Parliament Kevin Sorenson could see the human impact of the weather on the faces of the farmers he met. "I saw farmers and ranchers come in and break down," he said. "It's been heart wrenching. You can't imagine the sound of the grasshoppers crunching under your feet. I recall seeing a farmer, some 55 years old, with tears in his eyes as his cattle, recently sold, were being led away. He put his hand gently on his wife's shoulder and peacefully said, 'Don't worry honey, we will make it through.'"[4]

The drought of 2002 was an unequivocal disaster for farmers in the affected areas. The anguish seen on the faces of the usually resilient and independent-minded Western farmers was something Canadians had rarely seen before. These farmers were desperately calling out for help. Their situation was a stark reminder that hardship can strike us all.

What crops looked like in July 2002 in drought-stricken areas of Saskachewan.
Photo: Constituency Office of Carol Skelton.

Notes

1 Environment Canada "The Top Ten Weather Stories for 2002." www.msc-smc.ec.gc.ca. Environment Canada rated the top weather stories for 2002 based on the impact they had on Canada and Canadians, the extent of the area they affected and their longevity as a top news story.

2 Ibid.

3 Statistics Canada. "Estimates of production of principal field crops." *The Daily* www.statcan.ca 23 August 2002.

4 Johnsrude, Larry. "Rookie Alliance MP rides herd on Hay West." *Edmonton Journal* 18 August 2002.

Farming—Risky Business

Business failure in the private sector is a cruel and necessary fact of life. It remains one of the fundamental planks of a Darwinian-style free enterprise system that sorts good ideas from bad, hard work from sloth and, perhaps, good luck from bad.

The prospect of failure is a farmer's constant companion. Droughts, insects, floods, plant and animal diseases, and international trade disputes can all spell disaster, and most often none lie within the control of the individual farmer. Few other business people face as many uncontrollable variables as does the farmer.

There is nothing new in the conclusion that farming is a risky business. If the risks are well known to all and the logic of the marketplace is followed to its inevitable conclusion, why not let farmers sink or swim according to short- and long-term climate fluctuations and the ebb and flow of worldwide markets? If the survivors need additional protection from bad weather or adverse markets, why can't they insure for risks just like other businesses? Why must farming be reliant upon forms of government assistance?

When you talk to farmers, a proud and independent-minded bunch, you find they loathe any notion of reliance on government. They would be much happier to receive a fair price for what they produce and to use their savings or insurance to see them through the bad times.

The fundamental problem with free enterprise in Canadian agriculture is that the market is not free. The worldwide system of agribusiness is built around a long-standing, sophisticated and an often hidden system of income supports and subsidies. Simply put, international food production subsidies keep the prices for farm outputs artificially low. Because the farming industry worldwide abounds with subsidies, even the very best and most efficient of Canadian farmers could fail without a national system of income supports. Without some form of government income assistance, Canadian farmers would have no hope of competing in the global market.

Certainly farmers aren't happy with the current system. An economist might explain that all this balances out because low food prices are offset by higher taxes required to fund farm subsidies. The consumer pays more taxes but gets much lower food prices and a reasonable guarantee of a stable food supply in return. The farmer receives less than his product would otherwise normally command but presumably gets a stable source of income in return. Yet, despite farm income subsidies, farmers are not among the financially privileged, and many live perpetually close to the edge of financial calamity. Income supports, like so much else in government, work in theory but not always in practice.

Existing government subsidy programs that could presumably have been enhanced to respond to the drought in Western Canada in 2001–02 include the Net Income Stabilization Account (NISA). This voluntary program, developed jointly between producers, the Government of Canada and participating provinces, is designed to help farmers achieve income stability. It gives farmers the opportunity to deposit money annually into a NISA account in good years and receive matching government contributions. In lower income years, producers can make withdrawals from funds they have set aside. The complication facing drought-ravaged farmers, however, was that their NISA accounts are accessible only after they have determined their income for the year and have met certain eligibility criteria. The process is slow and not designed to meet situations of immediate need. In addition, while NISA is an attractive program for established farmers who have amassed significant money in their accounts, it is a program that is beyond the reach of many younger, less-established farmers. Beyond that, few farmers have enough accumulated financial resources to survive a severe or lengthy crisis.

Another relevant federal–provincial farm income support program is crop insurance. This cost-shared program stabilizes a farmer's income by compensating for crop losses caused by natural hazards, including drought. Farmers are insured on the basis of their previous production history. Again, this is a program that kicks in after the total loss is determined, usually at the end of a season, and then only after a complex series of calculations are made by adjusters. Western farmers knew early in the spring of 2002 that the drought would reduce crop yield to little or nothing. The best solution at the time would have been to turn their cattle into the fields so they could eat what little growth had occurred. Yet farmers had to watch what limited hay they had in the fields go to waste because insurance adjusters have to assess the loss before crop insurance pay-outs are made. Before many farmers could make a claim under the federal crop insurance program, they were forced to harvest their phantom crops in order to prove a loss to the underwriters from the government. This led to the farce of farmers harvesting fields containing virtually nothing. The cost of fuel and wear and tear on the machines far exceeded the value of the harvest in the field. But that is the way the crop insurance system works. Reasonable people exercising good judgment could have spared farmers much grief and cost if drought damage could have been assessed earlier than normal. It is is geared toward periodic shortfalls in production, not continuing or wide-scale disaster. It is simply not designed to cover total crop loss, which is what many Western farmers faced in the drought of 2002.

The data show that claims under crop insurance in 2002 from farmers in Alberta and Saskatchewan were three times higher than the year previous. This is a province-wide statistic. Claims in the drought-infected areas would have been even higher.

Beyond income support and insurance programs, government-sponsored farm disaster relief programs have been either ad-hoc or a small segment of farm income programs. Consequently, the farming community cannot depend on the timing, magnitude or effectiveness of disaster assistance. This haphazard response system has lead to the unseemly ritual that sees farmers and their advocates pleading for politicians to respond to situations of dire need. This crisis atmosphere has frequently shown itself in the Parliament of Canada. Of the nine emergency House of Commons debates since 1997, six have dealt with agriculture.

One of the many complications for farmers seeking drought relief is the question of what constitutes a disaster. There are no clear definitions or automatic triggers that signify a drought. A drought is an insidious process that eats away at hope ever so slowly until rain, if it comes, is too late to save the crops.

Despite government support through production subsidies and insurance, and despite the steely resilience and determination of Canadian farmers, many still fail. Sadly, bankruptcy and distress sales remain a part of farming life in Canada. In an emergency debate on the farm income crisis in the Parliament of Canada in 2002, Joe Clark lamented the sad economic state for farmers in Canada: "Since 1996, Canada has lost 30,000 farmers. The census on agriculture has confirmed that more and more producers are packing up their dreams and simply moving off the land. Farm debt has grown to $15 billion between 1993 and 2000. Over 4,000 Canadian farms have declared bankruptcy."[1]

Inadequate and unpredictable systems of crop insurance, income stabilization and disaster relief are what farmers faced when the drought of 2002 struck major segments of Alberta and Saskatchewan. It's no surprise that farmers felt the need to help one another. They knew there was no system in place to handle a crisis of this extent.

Farmers remembered another drought and shortage of hay back in 1970 when the government response was to issue coupons that farmers could use to buy hay. But by the time the coupons arrived, they were too late to help the farmers who were forced to sell cattle to survive.

When most businesses fail there is rarely a whimper from the community they serve. Bankrupt businesses are assumed to have been inefficient or to have failed to meet market demand. Farming is different. Farmers recognize how hard it is to make a living in Canada when international commodities markets or severe weather can beat even the best of them. What was needed in July of 2002 was a system to bring hay to animals—not in a year or even a month, but immediately. Based on experience, farmers knew that a quick response was not about to come from governments. This understanding instills a natural empathy and bond among farmers, who instinctively pitch in to help one of their own in a time of need. Everyone has heard stories of farmers banding together after a fire to rebuild a neighbor's barn. Farmers recognize that a failure means much more than an economic loss. What is at stake is a way of life.

As a postscript, the weaknesses in the government's farm income stabilization and disaster relief programs caused the Department of Agriculture to reform the system. Starting in 2003, the Canadian Agricultural Income Stabilization Program (CAISP) replaced the Net Income Stabilization Account (NISA) and the Canadian Farm Income Program (CFIP). CAISP provides both income stabilization and disaster assistance. The program is designed to respond more generously to those farmers facing the deepest losses. It is not known whether this revitalized program, had it been in place in 2002, would have provided a more timely and effective response to the drought in Western Canada than programs existing at the time. Hopefully, farmers will never have to find out how effective this new disaster relief program really is.

NOTES

1 Clark, Joe. *Hansard*, 37th parliament, 2nd session, edited, number 002, Government of Canada, 8 October 2002.

Friends from the East —
The McWilliams

A gang of proud farmers and other volunteers in Carlsbad Springs, Ontario in the summer of 2002 joyously lending a hand to help those in need.
Photo: Hay West volunteer.

The fact that most Canadians still remember the infamous bumper sticker epithet "Let Those Eastern Bastards Freeze in the Dark" some 30 years after it was first coined speaks to the long-standing resentment that many in the West have toward the East. At the time, the issue was oil, and more specifically the National Energy Policy that forced Alberta producers to sell oil to Canada at less than world market prices. Over the last generation, Western alienation has not gone away. The West may have expanded greatly in terms of population and economic wealth, but it has not enjoyed a corresponding increase in influence and power in the national government.

Coming into 2002, more Westerners than ever believed they gave far more than they got from Confederation. Poll after poll confirmed a strong level of mistrust among Western Canadians toward their national government, which they saw as dominated by Eastern Canadians. A 2002 Ekos opinion poll reported that Western disaffection was a real issue, particularly in Alberta and Saskatchewan. The sense among Westerners of belonging to Canada had declined sharply in the past decade, the Ekos study noted. As recently as 1995, between 94 and 97 percent people in the four Western provinces voiced a strong sense of belonging to Canada. Seven years later, that number had declined to between 82 and 86 percent.[1]

"Before the drought, many people on my riding association executive believed that separation was the right answer for what is wrong with Canada," remarked Kevin

Sorenson, MP for Crowfoot Alberta, one of the areas hit hardest by the drought. Sorenson heard about the problems with Confederation on a daily basis.

Yet, while feeling profoundly alienated from the rest of Canada, Western Canadians were generous in the support they offered to those in Eastern Ontario and Western Quebec paralyzed by the Ice Storm of 1998. The Ice Storm brought daily social and economic activity to a halt. Close to 100,000 people took refuge in shelters as electricity transmission was severely disrupted in some areas for weeks. The Canadian Armed Forces were dispatched to help in the largest peacetime deployment of Canadian troops ever. Farmers were not immune to the winter storm. While poultry and hog farmers struggled with improper ventilation and temperature fluctuations, the hardest hit were dairy farmers. Without generators, farmers couldn't milk their cows, which left them vulnerable to mastitis, an infection of the udder. Westerners, like others across the country, reached out sympathetically to those affected by the disaster and sent money and generators to those in need. Ultimately, it was the federal and provincial governments that delivered the decisive response to the Ice Storm. It was governments that coordinated the relief effort and invested millions of dollars to get services back on line and the local economies up and running.

The Red River flood of 1997 in Manitoba was another natural disaster that engaged the country and governments immediately. The "Flood of the Century" created an enormous 2,000 square kilometer inland sea flooding over 800 farms and forcing almost 25,000 residents from their homes. A massive army of civilians and military personnel was quickly mobilized to minimize destruction. Both government and community funding were quickly made available to those in need.

Canadians' understanding of the consequences of the Ice Storm and the Red River flood was instantaneous. The country could see the distruction and feel the despair in the nightly newscasts from the disaster areas. Governments and the population responded as one. There were no debates about what should be done or who should pay the cost. Whatever was needed was given.

But a drought like that experienced in Western Canada in 2002 is different than a storm or flood. A drought might be inconvenient to many but disastrous to only a few. It develops slowly and insidiously; it lacks immediate drama; and it is not particularly photogenic until all the damage has been done. Perhaps the sight of a gaunt, starving herd of cattle might have triggered some awareness of a national emergency, but farmers were more likely to give their cattle away than to have them suffer and die in the field. Carol Skelton, a Saskatchewan MP, calls a drought a "silent disaster."

The infamous bumper sticker that encapsulated many Westerners' feelings about Central Canada.
Photo: *Calgary Herald.*

Fallen trees on Park Avenue, Montreal, after the Ice Storm that paralyzed large portions of Eastern Ontario and Western Quebec.
Photo: Ioannis Rekleitis.

While the response to the Ice Storm and the Red River flood gave clear indication that Canadians were prepared to help one another in a crisis, it was not exclusively a case of the East rising to support the West. Canadians nationwide responded sympathetically with governments leading the way. When drought struck Alberta and Saskatchewan in 2002, the notion of a group of farmers from Eastern Canada, and in particular from Ottawa, coming to aid of some drought-stricken farmers in Alberta and Saskatchewan was unimaginable to some. That included members of Kevin Sorenson's riding association, some of whom were quite willing to consider giving up on Canada.

* * *

Morris, Manitoba, during the 1997 Red River flood.
Photo: Natural Resources Canada.

Wyatt and Willard McWilliams, farmers from Navan, Ontario, believe in Canada and in the spirit of the Canadian farmer. They also know all about helping people in need and taking on challenges few others would even dream about. Kevin Sorenson, and farmers from the West, had not heard of the McWilliams before the drought of 2002, but they were about to hear plenty.

Willard Thomas Edward McWilliams was born on December 30, 1936, one of seven children to Evelyn and Ira McWilliams He was raised on the family farm.

Following his father's sudden death in 1963, Willard assisted his mother with the operation of the family's century-old farm. Later, Willard and his wife, Mabel, purchased the farm beside the original Navan homestead, where they raised their five children—Wyatt, Wendy, Wanda, Wayne and Cheryle—all of whom, with the exception of Wendy, still reside in the Navan area.

Willard has been a farmer and lover of horses his entire life. For many years, he was an exhibitor in heavy horse shows at local fairs, including the prestigious Royal Agricultural Winter Fair held annually in Toronto. He was also a prominent horse breeder in the draft horse industry.

Willard has always been an active volunteer in his community. He regularly participates in annual parades such as the St. Patrick's Day Parade, Santa Claus Parade, the Canadian Central Exhibition Parade and local fair parades. He also instilled a sense of community leadership in his children. It was not surprising to Willard that his son Wayne personally resurrected Ottawa's dormant St. Patrick's Day Parade by unofficially taking a few decorated floats down some of Ottawa's busiest streets on the appointed day.

During the early 1980s, Willard donated and transported hay to drought-stricken areas of Manitoba. It was a year in which the East had an abundance of hay when the West had gone dry. The Government of Manitoba gave subsidies to farmers during the drought that allowed them to ship hay from out of province. The hay was moved mostly by train, although Willard took his hay to Manitoba by truck. Willard was impressed with government inspectors who let the hay roll even when transport rules were not being strictly followed. What was important was saving the cattle.

In 1995, Willard was the originator and a primary organizer—along with his family, the community, the Navan Fair Board and fellow horsemen—of the World Record 50-Horse Hitch held in celebration of the 50th Navan Fair. The event drew approximately 45,000 people to the small community, including the British Broadcasting Corporation, which recorded the event for the series *Record Breakers.* Willard gained official entry into the *Guinness Book of World Records* for being the single driver of the 50-horse team. The hitch was carried out a second time at the Rideau Carleton Raceway in 1998, an event that raised money for the Ice Storm relief effort in January 1998.

Wyatt and Willard McWilliams and the Guinness World Record 50-horse hitch on the streets of Navan, Ontario.
Photo: M. Sharpe.

Farming has been a part of the life of Williard's son, Wyatt, since the day he was born, July 19, 1958. Upon graduation from high school, Wyatt attended the Kemptville College of Agriculture and Technology, graduating in 1979 from the Agricultural Technology Program. Wyatt has operated his own farm business (Navandale Farms) since 1979, where he and his wife, Cheryl, have raised three children: Brenna, Megan and Tara.

Wyatt was raised to become an active participant and leader in farming and community organizations. He is a passionate advocate for the farm community in which he lives. His involvement has included a stint with 4-H and then with the Russell County Junior Farmers Association for 10 years, including serving as County and Provincial Executive Director and President. Junior Farmers is known for encouraging personal development, leadership and community involvement among the rural youth of Ontario.

Commitment, dedication and hard work with Junior Farmers earned Wyatt a place in the Eastern Ontario Junior Farmers' Hall of Fame in 1989. He was also one of four delegates in the Ontario Ministry of Agriculture and Foods Junior Farmer U.K. exchange program in the mid-1980s, which involved a nine-week exchange program to England, Ireland and Wales.

Like his father, Wyatt has considerable experience as a hay broker, which included a commercial operation that shipped compressed hay to Ireland in the mid-1980s by ship. The operation gave Wyatt an appreciation for the many issues involved in transporting hay across great distances and into regions and countries with different transportation and agricultural regulations.

What raises Wyatt McWilliams' story to another level is that, since the age of 34, he has been legally blind. He

Willard McWilliams, left, and Wyatt McWilliams on their farm with some heavy horses.
Photo: Chris Mikula, *Ottawa Citizen.*

suffers from *retinitis pigmentosa,* a progressive degeneration of the retina that affects first night and then peripheral vision and then progresses to a complete loss of sight. Wyatt never complains about his illness, nor does he let it stop him from taking on challenges.

The McWilliams believe that farmers need a voice in Canada. They are not shy about speaking about the challenges of farming, and they work tirelessly to find solutions to the problems faced by farmers. Rarely a day goes by when the McWilliams' are not heard to say, "If you ate today, thank a farmer."

Their long list of accomplishments in farming and community activism has given father and son the confidence that they can solve problems and help others. After the 50-horse hitch project, their friends came to believe they were capable of accomplishing just about anything. Their experience gave the McWilliams a network of volunteers—a group they aren't shy about calling upon for help. When their call goes out, even with ideas that might initially seem crazy, their friends take the request seriously. "People expect us to take on unusual challenges," says Willard with a chuckle.

While the McWilliams have taken on some high-profile projects, they are happiest when they can focus on the work and not the glory. Throughout the Hay West Initiative, they were relieved when members of the Hay West Board or its staff picked dealt with the media so they could focus on what they knew and liked best.

Notes

1 The poll was based on 1,798 telephone interviews. The margin of error for pan-Canadian results was plus or minus 2.3 percentage points with a confidence level of 95 per cent. The margin of error for provincial results ranged from 4.4 to 6.3 per cent.

Hay West Gets Rolling

Wyatt McWilliams has a very clear recollection of how and when Hay West got started. "It was really my dad's idea," he recalls. "He was watching the news and saw the plight of the farmers in Alberta and Saskatchewan. They had no hay, and our sheds were full—with lots more in the fields. We're in the hay business, but we couldn't start trucking out there ourselves. That wouldn't do any good. People were talking about helping, but nobody was doing anything. So we felt that if we contacted local politicians, and they made some calls to see if they could get trains, then we could start something."[1]

When the McWilliams first thought about starting a relief effort to help drought-stricken farmers, the goal was clear: deliver hay to Western farmers—not in a few months, but today, tomorrow and next week.

While it may have been commonly assumed that government bureaucracies would solve the farmers' immediate problem, the McWilliams knew otherwise. They knew that established government programs, such as crop insurance and income supports, would only kick in at the end of the year. Their worry was that, by that point, many farmers would already have been forced to cull their herds, and that would have been devastating for beef farmers who had invested 20 years or more in building a balanced herd.

The McWilliams could draw on a lifetime of experience cutting and shipping hay. They also knew Eastern farmers would donate surplus hay. The problem was getting it out

Farmers delivered hay to the rail yards by truck, tractor and flatbed. Often a group of farmers got together and formed a convoy to bring their donated hay to the rail yards.
Photo: Hay West volunteer.

Hay West founders, from left to right, Rob Jellett, Wyatt McWilliams, Phil McNeely and Willard McWilliams.
Photo: Hay West volunteer.

West. They reasoned that trains were the answer, but they didn't have any money and thought that the odds of CN Rail responding favorably to a direct plea from a few small-scale farmers were low.

Rather than call CN Rail themselves, they turned to the most influential person they could reach, their local City of Ottawa Councillor, Phil McNeely. It seems odd that hay farmers would have a city councillor, but this was the result of the 2001 amalgamation of 12 municipalities. Ottawa now has the distinction of having the largest agricultural economy of all major cities in Canada. Today, 90 percent of Ottawa's land area is in a rural setting, and its agricultural economy employs, directly and indirectly, more than 10,000 people.

McNeely knew the McWilliams well and had witnessed many of the successful community activities they had led. The McWilliams knew that Phil McNeely had a lifetime of political involvement and was well placed to reach Don Boudria, a federal cabinet minister and Leader of the Government in the House of Commons. Boudria was their local Member of Parliament, and he had participated in the 50-horse hitch at the Navan Fair.

Willard McWilliams called Phil McNeely's office first thing on July 17. The Councillor's Executive Assistant, Rob Jellett, answered the call. Willard told Rob that he had been watching *Canada AM* and wanted to help the farmers out West. Rob instinctively replied, "Great idea. How can we help?"

When McNeely arrived in the office a few minutes later, he was immediately informed of the McWilliams' idea for shipping hay out West. McNeely embraced the notion and called Boudria.

It would have been very easy for Boudria to brush off McNeely and the McWilliams by redirecting them to the Minister responsible agriculture. And, he also knew little about the logistics of the intended relief effort and had no idea if the McWilliams had the capacity to do what they proposed. Undoubtedly, politicians are flooded with requests to get involved in some seemingly bizarre projects. When McNeely asked what Boudria could do about getting some railcars, Boudria's first thought was that the idea of shipping hay by rail across the country was farfetched. "Something—I don't know what—made me stop and say, 'What the heck, I know Paul Tellier. Maybe he can help.'" Tellier, the former Clerk of the Privy Council, the federal government's chief bureaucrat, was the President of CN Rail.

It was still the morning of July 17 when Boudria called Tellier. When Boudria asked about CN donating railcars in aid of the drought, Tellier quickly said yes. "Sure we'll help. How many cars do you need?" replied Tellier. Boudria had not anticipated an immediate answer, let alone one that was positive. He had no idea how many railcars were needed, but the number 10 sounded good, so that's what he asked for. In that moment, Hay West was born.

At any point on July 17, Hay West might easily have collapsed. Had Phil McNeely not acted upon the call from the McWilliams, had Don Boudria not had the presence of mind to call CN President Paul Tellier and had Paul Tellier not supported the plan immediately, then there might not have been a Hay West.

What is amazing is that all these individuals recollect that they thought the idea was bizarre at the time, yet something urged them to give it a chance to succeed. Without the support of a few powerful people at the outset, it is unlikely that Hay West would ever have seen the light of day. Then again, the McWilliams don't accept the word *no* very easily and might well have started Hay West by some other channel.

With the green light that put Hay West on the rails, Phil McNeely's Executive Assistant, Rob Jellett, called on his many contacts in the press. Prior to joining McNeely's office, Jellett had been the assistant news director and morning news anchor for CFRA, Ottawa's news/talk radio station. As soon as word came back from Boudria's office that 10 railcars were in place, Jellett prepared a press release that he faxed that morning to all Ottawa media. Under the title "Local Farmers in Sarsfield and Navan are Planning to Ship Hay to Drought-Stricken Farmers in Alberta," the release quoted Willard McWilliams: "Prairie cattle ranchers, who have been in the business for generations, are having to sell off their herds because the drought has been so bad they don't have any feed for their animals." Phil McNeely added his comments in the release: "This is just another example of how the people in Sarsfield and Navan care about the farming community. Three levels of government are working together, and we didn't need a committee to study the idea—we just went out and did it." Those who wanted to help were asked to call Phil McNeely's office.

Within minutes, radio station CFRA began featuring the Hay West Initiative in its regular newscasts. Every 30 minutes, listeners in Eastern Ontario, many of whom were farmers, were made aware that a relief effort was underway. Local CBC television picked up the story and sent a reporter out to the McWilliams' farmhouse that afternoon. That night Wyatt described his plan on regional television.

Given that the McWilliams had just made the call to McNeely earlier that day, Wyatt's appearance on CBC television news was unexpected. Wyatt's wife, Cheryl, who was at the family cottage in Renfrew, was shocked to see her husband on the screen when she was watching the evening news. She remembers thinking to herself: *I go away for a few days and look what happens.* The vacation at the cottage with the kids was cut short, and she and the children promptly returned to Navan to assist with Hay West.

Broadcast media reporters were asking questions, and McNeely and Jellett were making up answers as they went along. The need for coordination and exchange of information among those involved became quickly apparent. A more formal organization was needed quickly.

The first official Hay West meeting took place on Parliament Hill on July 19 in the historic Commonwealth Room of the Centre Block. Don Boudria hosted the meeting, which included the McWilliams, McNeely, Jellett, local farmers Doug Woodburn and Gib Patterson, representatives from Agriculture Canada and CN Rail officer Sandra Wood. Plans were made to load the 10 railcars pledged by CN Rail at the Brockville, Ontario, rail yard, about 100 kilometers south of Ottawa.

The meeting went remarkably well. Tasks were efficiently and effectively allocated. Wyatt and Willard would deal with the logistics of delivering hay to the Brockville rail yards. Phil McNeely and Rob Jellett would deal with the media and get the fundraising started. Rob Jellett would also work with the railway. Since no one had any direct experience with this type of activity, they spent considerable time exploring issues that might go wrong. The representative from Agriculture Canada was queried to see if there were any regulations that would restrict the shipment of hay. They were told there were none.

A second press release went out two days later on July 19. Farmers were asked to bring hay to Brockville on July 25. Recognizing that the relief effort was in the beginning stages, Phil McNeely stated in the release: "At this point it's just a few hundred bales that won't do much to save the thousands of cattle herds, but we're hoping the Ontario and federal governments can work out a plan to ship thousands of tonnes of hay. Both CN and CP Rail have expressed interest in helping, but there are lots of details still to be worked out. There's no doubt the interest is there. The farmers want to help, but the Ontario and federal agriculture ministries have to carry the ball."

The first newspaper account of Hay West appeared the next day in the *Ottawa Citizen*. The story sketched out all that was known about Hay West at the time. Jellett admitted to the press that, as yet, there was no master plan. "We have no idea how much of the cattle feed will eventually be shipped to drought-stricken Alberta. It depends on the generosity of people in Eastern Ontario."[2]

Not long after the first meeting, the need for an identity and logo for Hay West was evident. In fact, the name *Hay West* came about simply because Phil McNeely needed to write a letter. In the absence of a name or letterhead, he pondered for a few minutes and came up with *Hay West*.

The official Hay West hat.
Photo: Bob Plamondon.

There were no discussions, no meetings and no consultation with his co-founders. It was simply done.

The Hay West logo had similarly modest and rapid beginnings. Wyatt McWilliams wanted a hat that he could hand out to volunteers and donors on July 25, so he asked for the help of his sister Wanda, who had been the creative force behind the 50-horse hitch logo. A few hours later the Hay West logo was ready, which was simply the words *Hay West* in the golden hue of hay.

While Wanda was designing the logo, other McWilliams' family members pitched in to help, including Wyatt's brother Wayne, who would spend the weekend loading and delivering hay.

The Hay West hat would become a valuable and treasured collectors' item in the farming community. It is remarkable that a symbol costing less than $10 could prove to be such valuable currency. Easterners who went West wearing the hat were said to be mobbed by grateful farmers.

Many farmers made up their own signs to proudly signal their connection to Hay West. Photos: Hay West volunteer.

While the Hay West hat became the official symbol for the organization, many farmers took great pride in coming up with their own homemade signs and slogans that graced their trucks as they delivered the first loads of hay to the rail yard.

Don Boudria was extremely encouraged by the early developments in Hay West and made Hay West a daily and important fixture in his schedule. If there were a Minister of Hay West, it would have been the Hon. Don Boudria.

As news spread about Hay West, others, both inside and outside of agriculture, wanted to get involved. Because Don Boudria's name was mentioned in many of the news clips, he started to receive calls with offers of help. Myron Thompson, MP for Wild Rose Alberta, heard about Hay West while watching the evening news. Through the Prime Minister's Office, Thompson tracked down Boudria at home on a Sunday afternoon. "I told Don how horrible the situation was and how desperate we were for help. I wanted to get involved." Boudria accepted the offer and asked Thompson to take the lead distributing donated hay in the West.

Months later Boudria recalled how Hay West helped him to get to know Myron Thompson as a colleague rather than combatant. "I had the impression he was not very progressive and would be difficult to work with. I was wrong. He was empathetic, practical and understanding. This was another case where Hay West helped to improve East–West relations."

The next meeting of Hay West was held at Ottawa City Hall, which became the location for most subsequent meetings. Don Boudria attended the meeting and recommended that Pierre Brodeur be brought in to help manage the operations. Brodeur had called Boudria to offer his help after watching the Ottawa television news story about Hay West. His experience was ideally suited to Hay West's needs: he was a former business executive with Bell Canada, a former dairy farmer from Quebec, a former small-town mayor and, most recently, the executive assistant to a federal cabinet minister. Brodeur's unique constellation of skills and contacts were welcomed.

The activity around Hay West through those early days in mid-July was like a beehive. Pierre Brodeur could see this when he escorted Wyatt in his first few days with Hay West as his driver, an essential function given Wyatt's blindness. The nerve center of Hay West, otherwise known as Wyatt's kitchen table, was out of control. It was clear to Brodeur that Hay West needed systems, structure and facilities to keep pace with how the country was responding to the relief effort. Brodeur's political connections came in handy when, after a few phone calls and meetings, the Government of Canada agreed to provide Hay West with a surplus office.

The days leading up to the July 25 loading of railcars at Brockville were a busy ones for the McWilliams. They had 10 railcars to load and no idea if anyone other than their circle of friends and contacts would supply hay. After making calls to line up a few loads of hay, they spent the rest of the weekend trucking hay from Ottawa to Brockville.

What greeted them at the Brockville rail yards was a scene that was truly magical. The excitement was palpable and the atmosphere was like a carnival. "It brought tears to me eyes," remarked volunteer Doug Woodburn. "Farmers were showing up in droves with hay, many with homemade Hay West signs." Local Ontario Provincial Police officers even got involved, serving as escorts for impromptu convoys of hay wagons with lights flashing and sirens blazing when required. One volunteer told Wyatt McWilliams how he called his wife at home to tell her about the incredible scene he was witnessing. "Turn on the TV. You have to see how phenomenal this is," he told her. "Which channel?" she replied. "It doesn't matter—every channel is here. Just turn on the TV and you'll see us."

July 25 brought with it many stories of incredible personal sacrifice and commitment. Bernie Pryor, a farmer from Howe Island, just off shore from Kingston, went so far as to put 300 round bales of hay on a ferry and deliver them to the mainland.

At the rail yard were boxcars, open flat beds and flat beds with rails, all of which posed different issues for loading. No one had done this before so the crew working at the rail yard had to learn what equipment worked best for each type of railcar and how to load the hay to optimize the number of bales per car. The large square bales packed best, but many farmers used the large round bale because they provided more protection from the elements when stored in the field and the equipment was less expensive.

What had happened in the first week of Hay West was beyond anything the McWilliams could have imagined. Everything exceeded their wildest dreams: the donated railcars, media attention and the outpouring of support from farmers. Absolutely nothing had gone wrong.

The support flowing to Hay West increased as the amount of media attention devoted to the cause in those first few days increased exponentially. Starting with a few reports in the local Ottawa media in mid-July, coverage eventually peaked with close to 100 nation-wide daily media hits. No one could have predicted that Hay West would become such a media phenomenon and would garner so much support across the nation so quickly. How could anyone have thought that a relief effort conceived in a farmhouse in Navan, Ontario, could command local, regional and national news for a matter of weeks? Wyatt McWilliams remarked, "The press made Hay West. Without them getting the word out, there was no way we could have received so much hay or support from government and the business community."

In drought-ravaged Central Alberta, the *Wainwright Review* was among the first to highlight the value for farmers in the growing interest from national media. "It is also good to see the mainstream media picking up on the farmer's plight. The more they look into it, the more perhaps public pressure will make guys like Jean [Chrétien] and Lyle Vanclief do more than fly over the drought-stricken areas to appreciate what the rural areas actually contribute to the country."[3]

Back in Ottawa, the amount of press coverage Hay West was receiving was not being lost on the staff of the

Smiles and good cheer prevailed at the Brockville rail yards as farmers and other volunteers pitched in to help load hay on the first day of operations.
Photo: Hay West volunteer.

Prime Minister's Office (PMO). The key PMO contact for Hay West became Marjory Loveys, Senior Advisor, Economic Development, Policy and Research. Loveys worked directly for Paul Genest, Director of Policy and Research. The Prime Minister's office thought Hay West was an initiative worth supporting, but made it clear that the Government did not want to get involved with any operation that was commercial in nature. Loveys noted: "We wanted to do what we could to enable the initiative. We wanted to support the voluntary part of the program. We all had great admiration for the people behind Hay West. It was neighbor helping neighbor."

The Hay West volunteers had originally hoped to have enough hay to fill 10 railcars, but the mountain of hay that showed up in the first few days at Brockville could fill close to 30 cars. Seeing that more railcars were needed quickly, Hay West once again called on Don Boudria.

Since there were no controls on the supply of hay, no one knew how many railcars would ultimately be needed. On occasion, Rob Jellett, who was still dealing with the railways, would raise the uncomfortable specter of having to

Hay being loaded on rail cars in Brockville.
Photo: Hay West volunteer.

torch the farmers' donated hay because there was not enough transportation available. No one wanted that—not the railways or the government. The press had become Hay West's most valuable resource to keep public support running high. The railways kept responding generously with pledges of more and more cars.

Then came a call to the Brockville rail yard. It was Rob Jellett, who had just been contacted by Agriculture Canada. "Wyatt," said Jellett, "we have a problem. We can't ship any hay out West." The problem was the cereal leaf beetle found in certain parts of Eastern North America, but not in Saskatchewan and Alberta. Unless the hay could be fumigated, it wasn't going anywhere.

Wyatt looked at the loaded railcars and thought about what had been accomplished over the past week. He thought about the hundreds of people who gave so willingly to Hay West. For a moment he broke down, then said to himself, "We can't let this stop us."

NOTES

1 Zimonjic, Peter. "A Eastern farmer by trade, a hero out West by action." *Ottawa Citizen* 18 August 2002, sec. A: 4

2 Gray, Ken. "Eastern Ontario farmers to send hay to West: Drought-stricken Alberta in need of area's bumper crop." *Ottawa Citizen* 20 July 2002, sec. D: 5.

3 Clemmer, Kelly. "No Longer East vs. West." *Wainwright Review* 20 August 2002, sec. A: 4.

Science Rules

When PMO staffer Marjory Loveys first learned that Government of Canada regulations had stopped Hay West railcars dead in their tracks, she had only one reaction: "Oh my God, no. We certainly didn't want to make it difficult for Hay West," she commented. "We made the decision very quickly that the government would take care of the cost of fumigation."

Marcel Dawson, Grains and Feed Crop Specialist at the Canadian Food Inspection Agency (CFIA) remembered how he first heard about Hay West. "Anita Stanger from Agriculture called. She said that the government was getting involved with this massive shipment of hay to the West and wanted to make sure there were no regulations on this from

CFIA. I immediately knew we had a problem because of the cereal leaf beetle."

Oulema melanopus L., otherwise known as the cereal leaf beetle, eats away at farmers' crops. The first North American infestation was reported in Michigan in 1962, and the first sighting in Canada was made in 1967 in southwestern Ontario. The cereal leaf beetle is now widely distributed throughout Eastern North America. The U.S. does not regulate the beetle federally, but certain western states, such as California, have import controls to restrict the beetle's access.

Wyatt McWilliams was stunned when he heard about the need for fumigation. "When we met in Mr. Boudria's office on July 19, we asked the representative from

Fumigation regulations required that trains already loaded with hay had to be sealed before the fumigant could be introduced.
Photo: Hay West volunteer.

watch for
the **Cereal Leaf Beetle**

The cereal leaf beetle.
Photo: Oregon State University.

Agriculture Canada if there were any issues regarding the transport of hay. We asked again at a meeting on July 22. Both times we were told we had a green light to go."

In the press release announcing the fumigation problem on July 25, Phil McNeely spoke of how disheartened it was to be delayed: "It means the hay will leave late and will arrive late, but at least it will get there. I feel sorry for the McWilliams and all the farmers who have been working for days getting hay into Brockville only to be told at the last minute that everything is on hold."

When Agriculture and Agri-Food Canada called Rob Jellett on July 24 and told him that the hay couldn't be shipped until it was fumigated, 27 railcars had already been loaded in Brockville. A lot of sweat had gone into getting the hay on the trains, and the news was devastating.

"I would like to have ignored the order and just gone about our business," observed Willard McWilliams. He took matters into his own hands and went directly to CFIA headquarters to work out the options. While on his way, he spoke live with Lowell Green on Ottawa News/Talk Radio CFRA. The press wanted to know each and every detail as this story progressed.

"The last thing farmers wanted was for a good deed like Hay West to spread insects and disease to another part of the country," said Williard. "No one wanted to take risks, either in the East or in the West. We just wanted to make sure the issue was real and that we didn't spend any more time and money than was necessary."

The governments of Alberta and Saskatchewan were also interested in the fumigation issue. No one, not the farmers or governments, were willing to take risks with the health of plants or animals. The West proudly boasts that they do not have any rats and were comforted by the fact that the fumigation procedure would also kill any rodents among the hay. One can imagine the response from Westerners if Easterners, claiming to be doing something they thought would be good for the West, contaminated their environment.

To determine how CFIA was going to manage fumigation, Marcel Dawson immediately called the CFIA field office in Belleville and asked that a representative visit the Brockville rail yard and report on the activity. The next morning an excited CFIA staff member called head office and described the scene to Marcel Dawson: "There are an incredible number of people scurrying around the rail yard working with a virtual mountain of hay. It looks like chaos down here." They wondered how fumigation would be possible in such a setting.

Everyone was working on solutions. Wyatt McWilliams called the Ontario Hay Association and asked for help. They had never heard of the regulations and were dumbfounded by the issue. He then called the experts at the University of Guelph to see if there was some science that could be mitigate the requirement for fumigation. But scientists need time to resolve issues like this and were unable to help.

"It was frustrating because we knew that hay had been shipped west for years without fumigation," said Wyatt. "CFIA knew about this as well, but did not have the resources to patrol the highways looking for infractions."

Although they were responsible for creating and enforcing the regulations that stopped the trains, CFIA very much wanted to help Hay West. They didn't want to get in the way, but as they say at CFIA, "Science rules." They immediately declared Hay West an HVI, an acronym for "High Visibility Issue." Over the course of a year, CFIA might encounter five to ten HVIs, so it was clear they were taking Hay West very seriously. When a HVI is declared, a war room-style emergency operation is put in place, drawing upon representatives from policy, operations and communications units. The war room met daily to ensure the organization was fully informed and could respond as expeditiously as possible.

It was not surprising to CFIA that the farming community was unaware of the regulations. They acknowledged that publication of regulations in the *Canada Gazette* hardly qualifies as effective communication. Marcel Dawson admitted this much: "Inspection is a problem. Whatever periodic inspections we put in place at provincial weigh scales are minimal at best."

The people working on the file at CFIA couldn't help but notice the media attention that the cereal leaf beetle was causing. While driving in their cars, they could hear local talk radio hosts deploring the "bureaucratic weasels" that were thwarting the good works of Canadian farmers. CFIA staff thought they were doing the right thing and were working as fast and efficiently as they possibly could, but the criticism still stung.

A string of rail cars wrapped in plastic must have been a very strange sight to passers-by.
Photo: Hay West volunteer.

At the first HVI meeting on July 23, CFIA Vice-President Larry Hillier told the working group to do whatever they had to do to get the trains moving without delay. The same day, CFIA operations staff Andrew Dawson and Steven Palisek gave a sole-source contract to Abell Pest Control to fumigate the loaded railcars in Brockville. Abell was on site the next day and the hay was fumigated and ready to roll on July 26.

While CFIA might well have set a record for bureaucratic response time, three days seemed like an eternity to Hay West. Pledges of hay were cascading in, and the

In most cases, the enclosed rail cars could be used to contain the fumigant, and only the doors needed to be sealed.
Photo: Hay West volunteer.

momentum was threatened because of the uncertainty over when the hay could be shipped.

The actual fumigation process was complicated and cumbersome. To be effective, the hay had to be covered and sealed with tarps before the fumigant could be used. Initially the fumigation companies didn't have tarps large enough to cover the mounds of hay bales. The process was a little less complex for hay being shipped by boxcars. The boxcar did the same job as the tarps, and once the boxcar was sealed with tape, the fumigation could take place within the car itself. Once the tarp or tape was removed, the gas fumigant evaporated, making the hay safe to use. To be doubly assured of the effectiveness of the fumigation process, CFIA placed some live beetles into a load of hay to make sure they died, just as they were supposed to. The process worked.

Compounding the logistical nightmare of having to tarp and seal the hay for fumigation was the requirement that fumigation occur only at temperatures of 5°C and above. This effectively meant that October was the last month that Hay West could operate.

After the initial load in Brockville was fumigated, CFIA issued a tender, inviting bids for fumigation from companies throughout Eastern Canada. Three different firms were ultimately awarded standing offers. CFIA staff remained on hand to view each and every fumigation operation and kept track of every shipment. They were in constant contact with Hay West.

The ultimate cost of fumigating all shipments from Hay West was $564,584. There were also costs for CFIA staff time, including a significant amount of overtime.

Spending a considerable amount of money on fumigation was fine as long as the fumigation was really necessary. Wyatt McWilliams was left wondering what good he could do with the half million dollars being spent on fumigation if it ultimately wasn't necessary.

As a postscript to the fumigation issue, CFIA reexamined its policy on the cereal leaf beetle. After a scientific review, it was concluded that, in addition to fumigation, a range of options could be used to deal with the pest. These options now include:

- storage of baled hay and straw in a manner to keep it dry for a period of at least 90 days between baling and shipping;
- compressing the hay or straw at a pressure equal or greater than 105kg/cm^2.

Had these options been available at the time, Hay West would likely have used the compaction method.

While the fumigation issue was an ordeal for Hay West, there was also one very positive benefit: media attention.

While the Hay West story was compelling in its own right, the drama added by uncertainty and delay was more than any media outlet could ignore. Because of the fumigation requirement, media reports were increasingly critical of the federal government for not doing more to help. While Government House Leader Don Boudria was certainly on the case, and Agriculture Canada Minister Lyle Vanclief had instructed his staff to do what they could to help, the press remained unconvinced that the federal government was doing enough. On July 24, CBC news aired the first national television report. The story, told by news anchor Peter Mansbridge, was about Agriculture Canada putting hay shipments on hold pending fumigation. CTV *News* also covered the fumigation story the next day. "It is the kind of thing that makes frustrations mount and tempers boil," Lloyd Robertson reported. "Government bureaucracy is getting in the way of a good deed from Ontario farmers to their counterparts in the West. The Easterners have been gathering hay to ship to farmers in the drought-stricken prairies. The first shipment was scheduled to start the trip west by train this afternoon, but a delay over standard fumigating procedures has pushed it back by several days—crucial time that could mean death for starving cattle."[1]

The amount of press coverage would prove key to increasing corporate and personal donations needed to keep the hay moving. In addition, the government might well have felt guilty about the whole episode, which may have influenced their willingness to fund more railway cars.

While Hay West organizers were frustrated by the delay, Board Chair Phil McNeely said, "It may have slowed us down, but it also put us in the spotlight. We gained a lot more attention and probably made the government feel a little guilty. They probably put in more money as a result."

In the meantime, as the news spread, farmers' from all eastern provinces began to contact Hay West with more pledges of hay.

Notes

1 *CTV News with Lloyd Robertson*. Toronto. 25 July 2002.

Hay Donations

Eddie and Genie O'Brien donated 34 bales of hay.
Photo: Peter Zimonjic, *Ottawa Citizen.*

When Farm Coordinator Cathy Willoughby was asked how she got so many farmers to donate so much hay so fast she laughed. Her problem, she said, was trying to deal with the overwhelming mountain of hay coming her way. Hay West, she said, was like a snowball that gathered momentum and size with each passing day.

Cathy became the "Hay Queen" of Hay West. As a beef farmer from Smiths Falls, where she farms 1,500 acres with 200 head of cattle, Cathy knew farming. She could see firsthand the bountiful harvest that blessed the East in 2002. "We had to cut our fields early and often; otherwise the hay would have been too heavy for the equipment we had on the farm." It helped that Cathy was a director with the Grenville Agricultural Federation, a role that put her in close contact with the Ontario Federation of Agriculture.

Cathy's involvement with Hay West began as a donor when she brought 18 large round bales to the rail yard in Smiths Falls in early August. A friend of hers, Charlene Renkema, had been working with Wyatt McWilliams, helping to keep track of donations and shipments. Cathy offered to help Charlene, and it was not long before her organizational and computer skills were quickly put to use. Wyatt immediately saw the benefit of having someone who knew both farming and computers. That was the beginning of Cathy's full-time occupation for the next three months as Farm Coordinator for Hay West.

Most of the volunteers who worked in the government-supplied office spent their days on the telephone. The phones at the Hay West office rang constantly, from 6:00 A.M. to 11:00 P.M. seven days a week. Most of the calls were from farmers wanting to donate hay. Other calls came from generous Canadians wanting to support the cause and from the media who were after every angle on Hay West they could find.

In the first week, the decision was made to commit Hay West operations to a database. Government employees were brought in to help set up a program in Lotus Approach, and the many Hay West volunteers were trained to use the system to input hay pledges. It was important to track the details for each hay donation since priority needed to be given to donations that could be loaded with the greatest convenience and at the least cost. Obviously, standing hay was less valuable than cut hay. Hay delivered to the rail yard was more valuable than what had to be picked up at the farm gate. As well, large square bales were prioritized because they could be packed more tightly on trains than round bales. The hay also had to be matched to the available loading equipment. Farm tractors could load flat bulkhead cars, but small, versatile bobcats were required to load boxcars.

The phone didn't always bring good news. Staff members heard the odd complaint from hay brokers out West who were angry that donated Eastern hay was interfering with the local hay market.

More distressing were the many calls from desperate farmers out west. One call stood out in particular. A farmer called to say he had just killed off most of his starving herd and was sitting in his living room with his gun on his lap not sure what to do next. While listening compassionately to the distraught farmer, another Hay West staff member called the RCMP and asked them to visit the farm. Thankfully, the intervention was successful, and while the farmer was initially upset about the RCMP visit, he subsequently credited Hay West staff with saving his life.

The emotional impact of the drought was widespread. Many farmers became depressed while waiting for rain. Dr. Ernst, a Saskatchewan General Practitioner, became so frustrated by the flood of farmers suffering from stress and depression that he circulated a petition asking the government to intervene and provide relief for the drought.

The Executive Director of the Producers Association of New Brunswick, Nick Duivenvoorden, explained why New Brunswick farmers pitched in to help Hay West. "Farmers that face this kind of [crisis] have done themselves in. Farmers who have reached the depths of despair are a danger to themselves and their families."[1]

While some farmers faced stress beyond levels with which they could cope, Hay West brought hope. And while Hay West staff sometimes felt discouraged, they were invigorated by the many cards and letters from Western farmers stating what the donated hay meant to them.

It seems that those giving the hay received as much or more satisfaction than the recipients. Eddie O'Brien, a farmer from Chapleau, Quebec, who donated 34 round bales of hay, was a local organizer for Hay West. "When your cattle are bawling and you know they need food, it sure feels good to give it to them. Giving hay is no different than what they did for us during the Ice Storm. There should be no boundaries when someone is in need."[2]

Stories of the determination of Eastern farmers wanting to do all they could for Hay West were easy to find. Eve Yantha from Renfrew, Ontario, told a story of a farmer delivering a load of hay in the early days of Hay

West: "When I was helping to load this hay in Brockville, a man showed up with a small cube van packed to the roof with square bales. Behind the van was a small trailer piled high into a pyramid with bales. And in the front seat, he squeezed in another two bales. When he arrived, he said, 'I wanted to bring my wife, but there was no room.'"[3]

The lead organizer of the Pembroke yard summed up the intensity many farmers felt: "I am going to keep the shipments coming in. I'll pile them as high as I can. If the government won't pay to ship it, I'll take pictures and send them out on the Internet to tell the world what is going on here. Cattle are starving, farmers are going broke and I'm not stopping no matter what anyone says."[4]

Over the four months in 2002 when Hay West was operational, 1,714 farmers from five provinces offered to donate hay. This included 75,703 large bales (round and square) and 33,760 small square bales. Just over half the hay that was pledged ultimately made it to the West. The availability of transportation made it impossible to achieve a 100 percent delivery rate.

By the time the Hay West Initiative was winding down, every province in the East had donated hay except Newfoundland—and that's not because of a lack of enthusiasm from Canada's easternmost province. Regrettably, transportation links from Newfoundland made a contribution completely impractical. Most of the hay—67 percent—was pledged from Ontario, where, in 2002, growing conditions were close to ideal. Quebec pledged 14 percent; New Brunswick, 11 percent; Nova Scotia, 6 percent; and Prince Edward Island, 1 percent. Most pledges included delivery of hay to the rail yard.

One might wonder how such a massive amount of hay could be pledged over such a short period of time to a cause and organization that was previously unknown to farmers. Wyatt McWilliams has an answer: "While it was a great cause, it was the power of the press that made Hay West.

They told our story every day of the campaign, and farmers and the rest of the county responded. It is as simple as that."

NOTES

1 Risdon, James. "8 rail cars of N.B. hay head west." *New Brunswick Telegraph Journal* 20 August 2002, sec. Provincial News.

2 Zimonjic, Peter, Andy Ogle and Larry Johnsrude. "The Heroes of Hay West—The East." *Ottawa Citizen* 18 August 2002, sec. A: 4.

3 Zimonjic, Peter. "'I won't have to sell my herd': Western farmers praise generosity of Ontario brethren." *Ottawa Citizen* sec. A: 1.

4 Zimonjic, Peter. "3 million needed to ship hay bales West: Federal government urged to assist as donation outstrip available railcars." *Ottawa Citizen* 17 August 2002, sec. A: 4.

The Lottery

The second hay lottery in Camrose, Alberta.
Photo: *The Camrose Canadian.*

While the McWilliams had a network of farmers throughout Ontario and a growing network in the other eastern provinces, their contacts in Western Canada were few and far between. Yet they needed to develop a system in Western Canada to distribute the hay—and they needed it fast.

Alberta MP Myron Thompson made the first contact from the West when he called Minister Don Boudria to offer help. Thompson then went to work and determined that the best rail depot to receive the donated hay would be Wainwright, Alberta. As he thought about it, Thompson realized that fellow MP Kevin Sorenson should be involved. "Kevin," said Thompson, "your area has been hit hardest of all. You should take the lead on this." Thompson met

Sorenson a few days later in a coffee shop to talk about how the Hay West relief effort might work when hay moved west.

Sorenson, a rookie MP, is also a farmer, and although he had great sympathy for the plight of farmers, he was at first uncertain about whether he should take a leading role for Hay West in Alberta. He wondered what pitfalls lay ahead and whether this was really what a Member of Parliament should do. Most of the people who advised Sorenson warned him that Hay West was a nice idea with a big downside. People kept telling him not to get involved, pointing out that he would disappoint more people than you would help, that there would be too little hay to make a difference and that the risks of failure were too high. No one thought Sorenson should take on the challenge.

Kevin Sorenson addressing a Hay West news conference in Navan, Ontario.
Photo: Hay West volunteer.

At the same time, constituents kept coming to his office to tell him of their hardship. With despair staring him in the face, Sorenson thought this was not a time for deep analysis. This was a time for action. He decided to do whatever was possible to help.

Sorenson realized that whatever amount of feed could be mustered by Hay West would be miniscule relative to the need. He knew he could never meet the demand. To be a success, he reasoned he needed to first draw attention to the severity of the drought and second move the government to do the right thing. Whatever that was, he wasn't yet sure.

The logistics of setting up a distribution system were overwhelming. Who should receive the hay? Should the criteria be based on need? Should the size of farm be an influence? Should some farmers be excluded from consideration? Should the relief effort be limited to beef cattle

Carol Skelton, MP for Saskatoon–Rosetown–Biggar, in a parched Rosetown, Saskatchewan, field at the end of July 2002.
Photo: Constituency office of Carol Skelton.

only? How would the hay get from the shipping destination to the farmers' barns? Sorenson had little time to plan. He also had no money and no organization. He was starting from scratch.

While Sorenson was dealing with the situation in Alberta, his colleague, Saskatchewan MP Carol Skelton, telephoned Hay West Chair Phil McNeely to offer her assistance. Carol, who farms about 2,500 acres with her husband, Noel, entered politics with the primary mission of giving voice to the sad state of farmers in Canada, many of whom were being driven from farming for lack of income. Her children were also farmers, and she wanted to help give them a future they could count on. In the summer of 2002, she could look out her kitchen window to see how bad the drought really was. She knew she had to get involved in Hay West.

Skelton brought in Nikky Smith of the Saskatchewan Cattle Feeders Association to set up a system for the distribution of donated hay in Saskatchewan. It was Smith that came up with the idea of the lottery as a way of allocating hay in the West. It was objective, simple and attention-grabbing. It seemed to be the only idea that was workable. As much as it was desirable to send the hay to those most desperate, there was simply no capacity among the organizers to assess need, let alone do it in a matter of a few days.

Local media quickly picked up the news releases announcing the lottery. Farmers by the thousands dutifully followed instructions and telephoned Sorenson's constituency office and the Saskatchewan Cattle Feeders Association to have their names included in the lottery. What had not been anticipated was the sheer number of calls.

To handle incoming calls in Alberta, three full-time volunteers were added to the regular complement of office staff

OTTAWA CI...

TUESDAY, AUGUST 6, 2002 · ESTABLISHED IN 1845

HARD TIMES AT THE CHOCOLATE FACTORY
BUSINESS, D1

SUPERSTAR SELLOUT
Why rock stars and movie idols think it's hip to shill.
ARTS, B5

WHY BU...
Market gu...
BUSINESS, D...

Hay West reaches grateful farmers

in Sorenson's office. The phone company, Telus, responded quickly and installed additional phone lines. The phones rang from dawn to dusk. "I went to the office at 5:30 A.M. one morning to get some work done," recalled Sorenson. "The phones were ringing as I unlocked the door and never stopped. Our office was taken over by Hay West, even though we had no budget to take on this work. Thankfully, everyone in the community contributed. There was always donated food in our office, and people were very upbeat. We were finally doing something. It was very heart-warming."

Some 3,500 names in Alberta and 5,000 in Saskatchewan were listed for the first lottery, all residents of the drought-stricken areas. The only exclusions from the draw in Alberta were relatives of Kevin Sorenson. "The last thing this venture needed was for my brothers and other relatives to come up big winners. They weren't too happy to be told they couldn't enter the draw, but I didn't think we needed that kind of attention for Hay West." The Saskatchewan Cattle Feeders also made sure that every name in the lottery was from a drought-stricken area.

To ensure the absolute fairness and transparency of the draw, the Alberta Cattle Commission conducted the lottery in Alberta, and a public accounting firm managed the draw in Saskatchewan. The look and feel of the draws was very official. In Alberta the names were written on slips of paper and placed in a large rotating steel drum. A large crowd assembled at the Norsemen Inn in Camrose, Alberta, for the draw.

The lottery draw attracted an unexpectedly large turnout. Farmers didn't need to be in attendance to claim their prize, yet many gathered simply to watch. It was as if what was happening wasn't supposed to happen, which made it all the more interesting to witness. There was magic in the air, and people wanted to see if some rubbed off on them.

One by one, the names were drawn. Local radio stations were on hand to cover the draw and announced winners live on the air. One happy farmer learned he had won while listening to the radio on his tractor. Winner Bo Arvedson happened to be at the draw when his name was pulled. Shouting with glee after his name was announced, he was pounced upon by the media like he was rock star. The draw was indeed a curious spectacle.

Alberta farmer Jim Hunter's statement about not having to sell his herd was the front page "above the fold" headline in the Ottawa Citizen *on August 6.*

A win was worth about 35 large bales of hay, a value with drought-inflated prices of somewhere between $3,000 and $7,000. That made for many ecstatic winners.

Winning certainly felt good. "I've never won anything in my life. You don't expect it, especially in a year when everything is going wrong,"[1] said 46-year-old Eugene Minailo of Willingdon, Alberta, a lifetime farmer who received 35 bales of hay.

Jim Hunter, from Entwistle, Alberta, said, "I am so happy because this means I won't have to sell my herd. For me, this is making all the difference in the world because I have a small herd. I wish everybody could have it, I really do. It just turned out that I am the fortunate one, and I am really glad."[2] For Hunter, the hay represented about two months worth of feed.

Kevin Sorenson and Nikky Smith had the happy responsibility of telephoning the winners with the good news. About 1,400 farm families won hay, 800 from Alberta and 600 from Saskatchewan. Every call was special, but for Sorenson one stood out more than the others. Upon hearing the good news, one farmer explained how badly he needed the hay, but not nearly as much as his neighbor, who might not make it through the summer. "Can I give my hay away?" he asked. That was another reminder to Sorenson that he had done the right thing by getting involved with Hay West.

After the first draw, Sorenson remarked that, relative to need, the hay coming West was still a "drop in the bucket." Wyatt McWilliams never liked that expression. "It was a big job, and the need out there is great," he said. "When we started this, we didn't want it to be just a gesture. We didn't want it to be a drop in the bucket. Maybe it took a lot of drops to make a difference, but we raised a lot of awareness." That awareness kept the hay arriving at the rail depots and kept the pressure for more railcars going. Because of the success in gathering and transporting hay from the East, second and third draws were held in each province.

The drop, it seemed, was getting bigger and the bucket, fuller.

NOTES

1 Zimonjic, Peter. "'I won't have to sell my herd': Western farmers praise generosity of Ontario brethren." *Ottawa Citizen* 6 August 2002, sec. A: 1
2 Ibid.

Getting the Feed West

Hay being loaded on the trains at the rail yards in Brockville, Ontario in the early days of Hay West. Photo: Hay West Volunteer

Many Eastern farmers could see rail lines from their tractors and couldn't understand why the trains couldn't stop long enough for them to throw on a load. But Canadian National and Canadian Pacific don't work that way. They worry about velocity, systems, safety and coordination.

There is a unique language and way of doing things in the rail business—a language that Hay West did not understand. Pierre Brodeur, who was managing Hay West operations, knew he needed expert help. He asked the railways if they could recommend someone to help the Hay West side of the operation. Enter Dave Cameron. Dave, a Smiths Falls resident and Hay West fan, was a 37-year veteran of CP Rail. As a freight rail specialist, Dave had even done an interchange stint with CN. He had the confidence of the railways and was perfect for the job of Hay West Rail Coordinator.

Since there was more donated hay than donated railcars, there was always a risk that commitments would be made that could not be supported by available railcars and funds. Hay West needed reliable and timely systems to keep track of both hay and trains to keep every bale possible moving west.

Dave Cameron kept track of the number of railcars used to ship hay. The railways got things started by donating first 10 and then 27 railcars, but that number eventually climbed to 187 cars. Other corporations such as First Energy funded 50 cars, and Molson contributed another

20. Fundraising concerts out west concerts bought 75 railcars while TransCanada Corporation and the Progressive Conservative Party caucus provided another 3. The federal government was persuaded to fund 376 railcars. All told, 711 railcars were donated to the Hay West Initiative. The Government of Canada wanted a daily update on how its donated cars were being used, and it was Dave's job to keep them up to date.

Expanding the list of loading sites was an important part of Cameron's job. This was critical to the success of Hay West because farmers from all over Eastern Canada wanted to participate. Transporting hay hundreds of kilometers from the farm gate to a rail depot was too great an undertaking for many farmers who wanted to donate. They needed loading sites closer to their farms. In an effort to expand the list of loading sites, Ottawa Central Railroad (OCR), a short line operator, was enlisted to provide facilities and services to Hay West. OCR owns approximately 200 kilometers of track from Coteau, Quebec, to Pembroke, Ontario. Eventually, Cameron would find himself tracking activity at 24 loading stations in Ontario, Quebec, New Brunswick and Nova Scotia. Smiths Falls, Ontario, earned the honor of shipping more hay than any other depot. Once the loaded railcars were sent west, Dave Cameron put on pressure to have them unloaded and returned east as quickly as possible to be reloaded.

One of Cameron's many challenges was dealing with the different cultures of farming and the railways. He knew it was difficult for CN and CP to have a bunch of "can-do" farmers roaming around their rail yards with light and heavy equipment. The railways are extremely safety conscious organizations and are uncomfortable in any situation over which they do not have total control. Thankfully, there

At one point the government offered up the Canadian military to help with the logistics of moving hay. Photo: Hay West volunteer.

Safety was a big concern for the railways and all Hay West volunteers. At this unloading site in Saskatchewan signs were posted to ensure regulations were followed.
Photo: Hay West Volunteer

was not a single accident or mishap causing injury in all of Hay West's operations.

CN Director of Public Affairs for Western Canada Jim Feeney could not say enough about the effectiveness and efficiency of Hay West operations. "This was an extremely challenging and unique project. We didn't have much experience working with hay, which was awkward to load and secure. It worked well because all our staff was dedicated to Hay West and because of Dave Cameron."

Feeney also reflected on the legacy of Hay West. "The railways helped to build Canada by joining a nation together. In a way Hay West did the same thing, and ironically used the railway to do it."

The railways and their staff were happy to be part of Hay West. Ottawa Central Railroad General Manager James Allen remarked, "Our staff loved working on Hay West. It was a great cause, and the people we met were true heroes."

Hay West was premised on rail transport, but once the trains were rolling, Wyatt McWilliams and Pierre Brodeur were curious to see if trucking could be an effective and economical alternative. Trucks offered the advantage of flexibility. Loading could be done at a dispatch center in a small town or village. Unloading could be done directly at the farm gate, saving a huge effort in Western Canada relative to the trains.

Trucking had not been part of the original Hay West plan, and there was no government sponsorship available to cover the cost. Thankfully, the goodwill generated by Hay West allowed Brodeur to obtain very favorable pricing from broker Truck Load Services Inc. on trucks returning empty to the West. Truck Load Services President William

A convoy of loaded trucks
heading west.
Photo: Hay West volunteer.

Robinson said that it was easy to find independent truckers who were proud to be part of the Hay West team, many of whom went out of their way to adorn their trucks with homemade signs. Truckers often stayed at destinations long after the unloading to take part in the celebration of good fortune and generosity. They also went out of their way to make delivery to the farm gate as fast and easy as possible.

The first trucks moving hay from Ontario to Western Canada were loaded on September 6 in Ottawa. The shipment was 1,100 large bales of quality hay produced on the Central Experimental Farm and donated by Agriculture and Agri-Food Canada. Hay grown by the Government of Canada, within the boundaries of the City of Ottawa, was making its way to Northern Alberta and Saskatchewan—as

unusual a circumstance as one could imagine. And the quality of the hay was reported by all to be superb.

Based on the success of the first few loads trucked west, the trucking operation picked up pace, delivering large square bales, primarily from Eastern Ontario, throughout the fall. Donations made by individual Canadians and corporations were used to cover the cost to send a total of 161 trucks west. This represented something less than 20 per cent of all hay shipments.

Farmer Jim Hunter of Entwistle, Alberta, west of Edmonton, waits for his train to come in.
Photo: Peter Zimonjic, *Ottawa Citizen.*

Delivering Hay in the West

As pledges of more and more hay came out of the East, coordinating the delivery in the West became well beyond what MPs Kevin Sorenson and Carol Skelton could handle out of their constituency offices. The job in Alberta was ultimately given to the Alberta 4-H, while the Saskatchewan Cattle Feeders Association (SCFA) took care of its home province.

Alberta 4-H staffers Bruce Banks and Susann McGowan were enthusiastic about Hay West from the very beginning. Alberta 4-H made sure that the donated hay went to the right people, at the right place, at the right time.

Bruce Banks speaks glowingly about the work that Sorenson and his staff did before they handed the job over to the Alberta 4-H. "It was amazing what they accom-

plished from a constituency office that was not geared up to respond to a disaster of this sort," he said.

Banks and McGowan knew full well about the severity of the drought, which was the only thing farmers talked about at the Ponoka Rodeo over the long weekend in July. "There was no hay to cut," said Bruce Banks. "It was toughest on those who had never purchased hay before. They had no contacts or sources of supply. These farmers paid top dollar—probably two or three times the normal price. It was hard to blame the producers since they didn't have much of a crop to sell so they needed every dollar they could get."

Connecting buyers and sellers of hay was assisted by an Alberta government initiative that created an on-line marketplace for hay, but both the prices and the shortage remained high.

The Saskatchewan Cattle Feeders Association likewise knew the drought and the farmers very well. As the 2002 drought worsened, the association's General Manager Nikky Smith was inundated with calls from farmers lamenting the lack of feed for their starving cattle. "It was simply heartbreaking to hear the stories," said Smith. "Over the summer, we did what we could to help, mostly by helping farmers find hay from Southern Saskatchewan and by lobbying government, but for much of the summer our impact was really small."

Then some local farmers started to call Smith about Hay West. "They heard about it on the radio and on television and wanted more information. We contacted Phil McNeely's office and passed along whatever information we could."

Initially, Smith was surprised that Hay West had so much momentum, yet no one had stepped forward to take responsibility for distribution of the hay once it arrived in the West. She realized that someone was going to have to take the initiative and believed her association was best suited to do the job. She discussed the issue with her board of directors, who expressed some concern that this might be too big a job for an already overworked association with only one full-time staff member. This was at a time when Hay West was looking at distributing only about 20 railcars of hay in Saskatchewan and Alberta. "I remembered all those phone calls from desperate farmers, and I knew we had to do everything we could," said Smith.

With the help of local Saskatchewan MP Carol Skelton, Nikky Smith began to sketch out a plan. "Everything went smoothly. Every time I asked for help, people gave more than I could have even imagined. I remember asking Rack

A railcar filled with hay ready for unloading in Saskatchewan.
Photo: Hay West volunteer.

Petroleum to help with unloading, and before I knew it they offered up siding, equipment and staff. They were amazing and asked for nothing in return."

In Alberta it took the 4-H about a week to set up a distribution system. After that, operations were reported as "smooth sailing." Recognizing the value in the good name of Hay West and Alberta 4-H, Bruce Banks wanted to ensure there were no controversies or improprieties. To protect the integrity of the system, he required all recipients to sign a contract confirming that they had at least 15 animals on the farm and that they would not sell the donated hay— although they were allowed, in turn, to donate hay to a more needy farmer.

What no one had anticipated was the ultimate size of the operation. What started out as a plan to deliver only a few railcars of hay turned into a huge undertaking with over 700 railcars and 100 trucks involved. As the initiative went from days to weeks to months, some volunteer fatigue inevitably

set in. "We couldn't keep asking companies to keep contributing, so eventually we received a grant from the federal government to cover some of the costs," said Banks.

The Alberta 4-H staff was very much "on the ground" and witnessed firsthand the impact that Hay West had in drought-stricken Alberta. Banks remarked, "Hay West did more for national unity than what any politician could ever do. Wyatt and Willard McWilliams are heroes."

In addition to its role in the distribution of donated hay across the province, Alberta 4-H and the Saskatchewan Cattle Feeders Association established many personal and professional connections, and the two organizations now have a close working relationship. Nicky Smith reflects, "What was great about Hay West was how it drew us all together, East and West, and brought together the people of Saskatchewan. When we got together at the rail yards, we ended up having barbeques and other social gatherings. I met many new friends who will be with me for a lifetime."

They also now know many more farmers from the East, none more special, they say, than Wyatt and Willard McWilliams.

Hay Recipients

Hay West was definitely a family affair.
Photo: Hay West volunteer.

Saving a family farm is a powerful outcome. Family farming is more than just a livelihood—it's a way of life.

While the hay shipped west could provide for the short-term needs of only 10 percent or so of the farmers who entered the lottery, all western farmers seem to have been inspired by the generosity of Hay West. There may have been a shortage of rain in the West, but there was abundance of hope and gratitude. Simply knowing that Eastern farmers knew their plight and worked hard to help must surely helped many affected farmers endure a long, dreary, dry summer.

Ottawa Citizen reporter Peter Zimonjic, at the scene of the arrival of hay in Wainwright Alberta, described the excitement that inspired Western farmers, not entered in the draw, to drive up to five hours to witness the Eastern hay arrive—even though it was destined for others. "The grand arrival was straight out of the movies," Zimonjic wrote. "The local politician standing in the back of a pick-up talking to the crowd of gathered farmers over a megaphone. The farmers hugging each other. The small children holding homemade signs saying, 'Thank You, Ontario.'"[1]

Perhaps the most poignant way to express what it meant to receive donated hay is found in the words of the farmers themselves, many of whom sent a card or letter to Hay West.

The Schwartzs, from Winfield, Alberta, wrote about how difficult it had been to find hay and feed for their cattle and how the donated hay would help them keep going:

Children from Wainwright welcome the CN train as it comes into the station in Wainwright, Alberta.
Photo: Kelly Clemmer, *The Wainwright Review.*

To All Our Good Ontario and Down-East Friends and Neighbors,

Thank you so much for the load of hay we won in the Hay West lottery. We couldn't believe our luck when they phoned us. To make it even nicer, we only had to drive about 15 minutes from home to pick it up at the 4-H Center.

We have 106 head of cows on shares with my brother. . . . We ran them up in Central Alberta for most of the summer where we live. We ran short on grass so had to haul 35 pairs down south of Calgary ($900 trucking bill) July 18 and rented some grass down there. Were able to keep the rest until September 26, then hauled two more liner loads down. . . . Another $1800 trucking bill, and we are paying $20 a cow/calf pair. Looking for more grass or stubble. We also got 300 acres to cut and bale down where the cows are if we can get it. It is four hours south of home. My husband

is down there now cutting. . . . If we are lucky enough to get it before it snows, we will haul the bales and cows back up here to calve them out in February. Will sell the calves the end of this month, we think.

So you can see what a tremendous help the hay is. We got about 50 bales of our own off 45 acres, so with the 25 we won we will have enough to feed for almost two and half months. . . . Just praying it will rain next year.

This truly has been a "Year from Hell" in our area, but . . . we are thankful for [the help] and our families and health.

Anyway, just wanted you folks to know how very much we appreciated your generosity and hope to be able to return the favor sometime.

–Bob and Gloria Schwartz

Laura Towers from Alliance, Alberta, wrote about the emotional lift the Hay West Initiative had brought to her family:

To the donors and organizers and other volunteers,

We send you a huge thank you for this wonderful project you have organized. The generosity of the farmers who have given their hay free of charge to those of us who are in need is absolutely awesome. When we first heard of the project, we were excited and grateful, even though we little expected to be the beneficiaries.

Early in July we reduced our herd by one half, and were wondering if the rest would have to go as well. I received word about noon on the day our son's name was drawn in Camrose. When my husband and son came in for lunch, the looks of joy and relief on their faces were something worth seeing and remembering for a long time. They had just been discussing ways of making it through the winter, and the news of our good fortune was great timing. The amount of hay we received on September 25 is exactly the amount we needed to make it till spring.

Thank you to everyone who contributed in any way. It won't be forgotten—and remember, what goes round, comes round!

—With gratitude from one farmer to many others,
Dave, Dennis and Laura Towers

Others, like the Swobodas from Meath Park, Saskatchewan, and Ed Pough from Dorothy, Alberta, were battling more than the drought. The Swobodas had to cope with a fire that burned their barn. Ed Pough had recently lost his wife. Both wrote letters that touched the hearts of Hay West volunteers:

Dear Saskatchewan Cattle Feeders Association,

We are small farmers, and the load of hay will help us to stretch the frozen canola we managed to bale up from a friend. We had a fire that burned our last year's hay and straw in the spring, so that with the poor yields from this year's hay crop, we were in sad shape. The donated hay from those big-hearted farmers from back East and your efforts to help have made a big difference and taken a load off our minds for this year. We will be able to save our main herd and not have to sell the calves before they are ready. Thank you and God bless. The hay was very good hay.

—Gloria and Morris Swoboda

Dear Hay West,

Picked up our load of hay—it's real good food and easy to handle. We have sold over half of our 400 head cowherd. This is a big help to feed the remaining herd. Have bought some feed, which we had to haul in from a long distance.

Thank you everyone for the support and the doing. We have been ranchers for all our lives; I just lost my wife who came from Parkhill, Ontario. If you are ever out this way, drop in.

—Ed Pough

The Wilkinsons, from Livelong, Saskatchewan, wrote a thoughtful, eloquent and appreciative letter noting how the spirit of helping inspired by the Hay West Initiative spread beyond those receiving hay:

Dear Hay West,

We received our load of hay today, which we are so grateful for. As I watched the truck come up the road, and saw the bales, I found myself wondering about the families who were responsible for this abundance.

I think about how strange it will be for our buffalo to eat hay from so far away. I give thanks to all these people who produced this feed so far away from our land. I also give thanks to all others who made it possible—those in the offices, those driving the trucks and the others who donated money for the incidentals and also those who have contributed in ways I am not even aware of.

The trucker who hauled our hay has a family. His wife and three children accompanied him today on his trip. Two of the children were kept home from school today because their parents wanted them to go to the rail yard to see this wondrous event. For them it was a grand holiday, a trip with their mom and dad, a packed lunch, and a chance to see Canadians supporting each other during hard times. What a great way to spend a day! This family usually has income from hauling grain; but there is no grain, so they, being resourceful, have been hauling hay. I give thanks that we have picked this man to haul our hay, which helps them as well. This drought and this project touches so many.

We would like to give a personal view of this gift. We live in west central Saskatchewan. There is little hay available this year, and it is for us the second year of drought. We raise buffalo and have for 23 years. We have at this time approximately 85 cows with calves and about 50 yearlings. Last year we used 400 bales to get through the winter. We had to start feeding early and had to feed late. We have in the past month been very fortunate to receive two inches of rain, which is the most all year. It helped the pastures immensely and may help with the green feed, if the frost holds off. We have been able to secure green feed from the south of the province and will truck it 400 miles.

The Hay West project is such an amazing psychological gift. We will have to find more feed, but the pleasure we have in receiving these bales is a yummy feeling.

–*Kevin and Judy Wilkinson*

The Velthuis family from Alberta wrote to express the sentiment at the heart of Hay West. They were hurting from the drought, but not as much as one of their neighbors, so they, in turn, gave away the hay they won:

Dear Hay West,

Last week we received a load of wrapped square bale silage. We would like to thank you for the bales. We gave the load of silage bales to a neighbor who needs the feed more than we do. He has about 400 sheep, and he has to sell about half of them because of lack of feed. These donated bales will help him keep sheep that he was otherwise going to sell. Included in this envelope is a card. We would appreciate it if you would send the card to the person who donated the silage bales.

–*The Velthuis Family*

Hay West helped to remind farmers that they live in a tight-knit community, where people reach out to help one another, a fact noted in a letter from the Goodfellow family from Neilburg, Saskatchewan:

Dear Hay West,

Earlier this month we were fortunate to receive 40 bales of hay in the Hay West lottery. We wanted to say a big thank you to everyone involved who helped out, especially those donating hay. Even when this generous offer was first announced, it did a lot to buoy our spirits with the fact that farmers in another part of Canada were willing to help us out. It makes you feel an affinity with all those involved with Canadian agriculture. . . .

So as we head into winter we are hoping, of course, for lots of snow and ample rains next summer. Then the memory of the "super drought" will be mostly a bad memory—lightened only by the fact that the farming community in Eastern Canada were there with a helping hand. Thanks again.

–*Glenn and Betty Anne Goodfellow*

The people who received hay were grateful, but so too were the people who gave. How true it is that anyone who is in a position to give should also be thankful.

The Chambers wrote from Chesterville, Ontario, about how inspiring it was to be a part of Hay West:

Dear Mr. McWilliams,

We wanted to wish you and your family a Merry Christmas and nothing but the best for the New Year! What an accomplishment to have helped so many. We are so proud to have been able to donate hay, and we are so very, very proud of you, your son and your family. Tears came to my eyes with every newspaper or TV news clip. We are so blessed here, and we were so honored to help. We just want to say thank you. Thank you for inspiring us all.

–*Chris and Susan Chambers*

Many other letters spoke of what Hay West meant to the unity of Canada, like the letter from the Wieler family from Carlton, Saskatchewan:

Dear Farmer Friends in Eastern Canada,

Words cannot express how truly grateful we are for the feed that was supplied by our friends to the East. Canada is a country of peace and unity—one that believes in "helping thy neighbor" whether world- or nationwide. We feel very fortunate to have such wonderful, giving neighbors in this great country of ours. I think we can speak for all farmers in Western Canada when we say thank you for your help in this, our time of need.

—Paul and Alice Wieler

More than national unity, the Glylanders from Alberta thought Hay West was a great humanitarian gesture:

Dear Hay West,

Thank you so much for your generous gift of hay. It has come in very handy for us and has made a real difference, as we will now be able to keep a few extra cows over the winter.

There are hard times all around us. Many of our neighbors have had to sell off most of their herds. It was so nice of you to donate like you did. It has restored my faith in mankind. And some day we will pass on the favor if it is needed and we are in a position to do so.

We are just a small farm and are starting out in cattle. We live just one hour west of Edmonton. Thank you again. God Bless.

—Rick, Gisele, Zachary, Jeremy and Geneva Glylander

Many letters were received from local town councils, some of which included a cheque in support of Hay West:

To all Hay West Participants:

On behalf of the Municipal District of Bonnyville No. 87, I wish to send sincere thanks to the organizers, sponsors, agricultural producers, suppliers, truckers and hundreds of volunteers that have made Hay West such a resounding success.

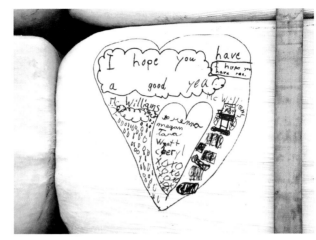

Many of the wrapped bales of hay were adorned with messages of goodwill, handwritten from the children of the farmers that made donations.
Photo: Hay West volunteer.

The thousands of tonnes of feed that have been shipped West to help farmers and ranches feed their livestock during the summer and winter season is greatly appreciated and will help to preserve breeding herds for years to follow.

The generosity of all those involved in the project shows the desire that Canadians have to help each other in times of need, and the spirit of sharing that has come through is something that all Canadians can be proud of. It is nice to know that the farmers from Eastern Canada understand the concern and devastation that poor crops have on the livelihood and the well being of their fellow Canadian farmers in western provinces. A special thank you goes out to the founders of the Hay West Initiative, Willard and Wyatt McWilliams of Navan, Ontario.

—Eva Urlcher, Reeve and Agricultural Producers in the Municipal District of Bonnyville No. 87, Bonnyville, Alberta

As Christmas approached, many Western farmers sent cards to Wyatt and Willard McWilliams. Many messages were filled with renewed hope that farming life would continue as a family affair, like the one received from Alberta:

Merry Christmas!

Thank you so much for the wonderful gift of hay. The feeling that so many people care is overwhelming. We live right next to Highway 16, which is one of the main links to Alberta and the drought area. Every day of the week the loads of hay and straw continue to pass through.

Hopefully next year will be better. Your thoughtfulness, concern and caring have already made looking forward to next year more positive. All we hope for is that people can remain on their farms and provide a living for their families. If your thoughtfulness can provide such a tremendous feeling of caring to so many, just imagine what we can do as a united country. It goes to show that nothing is impossible if you believe in your fellow man.

We feel very fortunate to live where we do as we believe this country was built by farmers like you. If one day you would have such a misfortune strike you, you can be assured we would be there to help you! It's such a good feeling to know you are not alone.

Thanks again and have a Merry Christmas. Best wishes for the New Year.

–Darwyn, Pam, Jesse, Rovynn, Emma and Dmika

People who watched the progress of Hay West on television responded with encouragement and money:

Dear Hay West,

Thanks for making it possible for me to help our Western farmers. Bless all our farmers who are giving so generously of their time and hay.

–Mrs. Frances McKean
Ottawa, Ontario

Dear Mr. McNeely,

Bales of hay arriving at the farm of Vernon and Lynn Priest in Lloydminster, Saskatchewan.
Photo: Vernon Priest.

Your effort in organizing this relief effort is commendable. Thank you. I am not from the West, nor am I a farmer, but it is truly wonderful to see Canadians help fellow Canadians in times of need.

–Doreen Lafleur
Kanata, Ontario

The impact of Hay West encouraged high-ranking officials to write to Hay West expressing what, at an emotional level, the effort had meant:

Dear Wyatt and Willard,

I cannot begin to tell you the emotion I felt when I heard that you were spearheading a project to have hay shipped to the prairies to help the livestock producers in Western Canada who are facing a shortage of feed.

Our country stretches from the Atlantic to the Pacific, and many Canadians never have the opportunity to travel outside their own province. Although there are thousands of miles between us, it is heartwarming to see the community spirit come to life when there is a need. It makes me proud to be a Canadian and to know that, as a Nation, we do support each other in a very real and tangible way. I want you to know that you have made a difference. Through your efforts, I would venture to say that Canada is a better place to live . . . for all of us.

Thank you for your incentive and for caring. Please know that your kindness and your compassion are greatly appreciated.

—*Dr. Lynda Haverstock*
Lieutenant Governor
Province of Saskatchewan

Perhaps no expression of thanks was more welcomed and heartfelt than the one received from Jacklyn Byers and Jess Valleau, two grade seven students from Wainwright Junior High School in Alberta. They traveled to Williard and Wyatt's hometown of Navan, Ontario, with their teacher, Curtis Hoveland, to present their card of thanks directly to Hay West organizers, Crowfoot MP Kevin Sorenson, government House leader Don Boudria, and Canadian Pacific and Canadian National railways representatives. The students had been involved in a class project on moral intelligence studying the concept of empathy. They thought Hay West was a good example of what they were learning. The Wainwright region had been among those hardest hit by the drought and had served as a hay distribution center. The card, more than a meter in size, and had been signed by 3,000 residents of the community.

The letters of appreciation continued to arrive for a year after Hay West sent its last shipment of hay. For example, an article in the Thanksgiving Day edition of the 2003 Stratford *Beacon Herald* looked back on the significance and lasting impact of Hay West:

The arrival of hay in Killam, Alberta, attracted the attention of the media as well as lottery winners.
Photo: Hay West volunteer.

"Martin Ritsma is going to miss Thanksgiving dinner for the second year in a row, but he's not complaining. . . . But the Stratford NorthWestern Secondary School teacher and part-time farmer can't help but think back to one year ago, when he and friend Marvin Good spent Thanksgiving on the road during a 30-hour, 5,000-kilometre marathon drive to Saskatchewan and back to deliver a truckload of hay to a needy farmer.

"The 63 bales were the last of the local Hay West campaign spearheaded by Mr. Ritsma, which sent 30 railcars full of hay to the prairies. Farmers from across Central and Eastern Canada shipped surplus hay West to help desperate, drought-stricken Western producers. . . . Thanksgiving is an appropriate time to reflect on unity the Hay West campaign afforded Canadians and also the importance of being self-sufficient in food.

"We have to make sure that we maintain family farms so that we have food that's produced in Canada," he said, adding that support for farmers should be a priority for local, provincial and federal governments.

'I have been inspired by you and the others that helped. When we get our feet back on the ground, I hope that we will be able to return the favor by helping someone in need,' Rosemarie Hemmelgarn said in the letter, which also criticized the lack of government support for farmers.

'Thank goodness that farmers look out for other farmers. Farmers would have encouragement to continue if the leaders of our country reached out to us like the people that organized the Hay West campaign and the farmers of Ontario that donated the hay,' she said."[2]

The many hundreds of heart-warming letters gave evidence of how Hay West had made a difference. The West was grateful. The East was grateful to help.

A great big thank-you card from the students of Wainwright Junior High School given to Wyatt and Willard McWilliams by Jacklyn Byers and Jess Valleau at the Meadowview Public School in Navan, Ontario. Wyatt's daughter Brenna is in the foreground.
Photo: Hay West volunteer.

"Mr. Ritsma tucked notes of encouragement into some of the bales he donated to the campaign. A farm family from St. Walburg, Saskatchewan, near Lloydminster, found one of them on the floor of their barn and wrote back with a thank-you letter this summer.

Children from Navan, Ontario, were keen to send messages of encouragement west on wrapped hay bales— on this occasion, at the closing ceremonies for Hay West on October 31, 2002.
Photo: Hay West Volunteer.

NOTES

1 Zimonjic, Peter. "'I won't have to sell my herd': Western farmers praise generosity of Ontario brethren." *Ottawa Citizen* 6 August 2002, Sec. A: 1

2 Shypula, Brian. "Thanksgiving Brings Memories Of Last Year's Hay West Campaign." Stratford *Beacon-Herald* 10 October 2003, Sec. A: 7.

Hay West Governance

Hay West was born in a crisis, hardly the atmosphere in which short, medium and long-term business plans take shape. By default, the plan in the initial days was to attack each obstacle that arose using whatever contacts and resources could be brought to bear.

The people who got Hay West on the rails constituted the initial informal decision-making structure. They were Wyatt and Willard McWilliams, Ottawa City Councillor Phil McNeely and his Executive Assistant, Rob Jellett. For the first week or so of operations, each of the four founders accepted the other as having authority to speak on behalf of Hay West and make decisions.

At the outset, no one knew what Hay West would become. The effort might well have started and finished with the first 10 rail cars of hay being shipped to the West. At the time, it would have been difficult to think otherwise. After all, there was no money in the bank, and no one knew if those first railcars represented the limit of what would be donated. Perhaps the only thing the founders felt they could count on for sure was donated hay from farmers in Eastern Canada.

From the moment that Hay West was first mentioned on radio, offers of financial support came flooding into Wyatt McWilliams' home and Phil McNeely's municipal office. Hay West's operations grew exponentially and it wasn't long before the level of activity put Hay West in danger of spinning out of control. Regular planning meetings, a formal structure of governance, decision-making and communication were needed.

There is nothing like long and arduous meetings to instill discipline and structure into an organization.

One of the first governance tasks was to make certain the finances were under control. With offers of financial support pouring in, people didn't have to be solicited to contribute to Hay West. What was needed was a mechanism for collection. This was initially provided through the work of Clive Doucet; another Ottawa councillor who had experience in fundraising and in directing charitable organizations and relief efforts. Doucet labeled his effort "One for the Road" since donated funds were used primarily to offset the costs of transporting hay. Chartered Accountant Bob Plamondon was brought in to set up a financial control and reporting system, and also to provide advice and management support to the organization.[1]

Hay West was not a charitable organization and could not issue tax receipts. The time and complexity associated with obtaining charitable status was incompatible with the deadline of shipping hay in a matter of weeks. While the organizers were mulling over this issue, Humane Society of Canada (HSC) Chief Executive Michael Sullivan contacted Councillor Doucet and then met the Hay West team to talk about how the two organizations could work together.

Sullivan suggested that HSC be authorized to collect donations on behalf of Hay West and then issue tax receipts to donors. While following the provisions of the Income Tax Act, HSC would pay bills submitted by Hay West for transport and other related costs. Time was short and this seemed like an ideal arrangement when first struck.

As it turned out, HSC was not what Councillor Doucet and the Hay West group thought it was. This was revealed when logistical arrangements were being made to announce the fundraising plan to the media. It became evident that

Hay West Chair Phil McNeely receiving an award on behalf of Hay West from Saskatchewan MP Carol Skelton.
Photo: Constituency office of Carol Skelton.

the HSC was not directly linked to the humane societies that deliver services to local communities. Discussions with the local Ottawa–Carleton Humane Society revealed that they had no affiliation with the HSC and that their national organization was the Canadian Federation of Humane Societies (CFHS). Doucet thought he had been dealing with a national organization with offices and clinics in every province. This national structure was the structure that Doucet had in mind for fundraising, and as a consequence, the plan to work with the HSC was cancelled.

With no time to waste, Councillor Doucet set up another fundraising framework. In a matter of hours, he struck a deal with the Canadian Federation of Humane Societies. Of note, this agreement was between Doucet and CFHS; Hay West was not a signatory. Further, there was no written agreement between Doucet and Hay West. In large part, people were acting on good intentions and verbal understandings.

The Doucet deal with CFHS gave them status as the prime charitable receiving agent that would issue tax receipts for all contributions and disburse funds as intended by the contributor, all within the regulations prescribed by the Income Tax Act. For this service, CFHS received a fee of 5 percent of contributions. CFHS was also the entity used by the Government of Canada to manage its financial contribution toward Hay West's administration costs.

When the 5 percent fee was agreed to, the Hay West organization had no idea of the amount of money that would ultimately be raised. This included a single donation of $200,000, which on its own this donation generated a fee to the CFHS of $10,000.

Other pressing issues included establishing Hay West as a legal entity. In its earliest days, when people would ask about Hay West, there was not much more to say than it was Wyatt and Willard and a few others operating from a kitchen table in Navan, Ontario. This made it awkward for people and organizations to do business with Hay West, especially those that did not need a tax receipt and wanted to give money directly to Hay West, thereby avoiding the 5 percent CFHS administration fee. To make this happen, Hay West needed a bank account, which meant Hay West needed legal status.

Another issue solved by having a legal identity was that of legal liability. If there were an accident at one of the loading sites, who would be financially at risk? The four founders? The Government of Canada? The rail company? In order to acquire insurance, there needed to be an organization. The response to these issues was to incorporate as a federal not-for-profit entity, and letters of patent were granted to the Hay West Initiative on August 19, 2002. The founding members and original board of directors consisted of Wyatt and Willard McWilliams, Phil McNeely and Rob Jellett.

Public liability insurance was not easy to secure, which caused some board members to consider resignation. Finally, a broker friendly to the farming community and an active participant in Hay West, Norman Blodgett of Darling Insurance, arranged for coverage when others could not.

The spirit of giving that Hay West inspired seemed to be everywhere, even in the legal community. The procedures for incorporation, which usually take weeks to complete, were processed in a matter of hours. The clerk at the Registry Office came in from her holidays to process the paperwork. The legal firm of Gowlings, and its solicitor, Pierre-Paul Henrie, donated their services and completed the paperwork in a matter of hours. Everyone seemed to understand the urgency of the initiative, and no one wanted to do anything to slow momentum.

Once incorporated, Hay West expanded its contacts and expertise by adding to its board of directors. Newcomers included Dal Brodhead, a businessman with experience in farming and community activity; Lloyd Craig, a farmer and supporter of Hay West with experience in community organzations; Wiebe Dykstra, a New Brunswick farmer who was leading Hay West activities in New Brunswick; Gib Patterson, a well-known Ottawa farmer and entrepreneur; and Doug Woodburn, a farmer and early supporter of Hay West. For a time Cuckoo Kochar, president of a large Ottawa-based homebuilding company, served on the board but could not continue due to time constraints.

With formal governance and communication structures now in place Hay West could offer much greater clarity and accountability, both externally and internally. On financial issues, governments could deal directly with Hay West rather than through CFHS. The general manager of Hay West, Pierre Brodeur, now had a board of directors to whom he reported.

Still, Hay West was a brand new organization without a track record or evidence of internal controls. This was a concern to the Government of Canada, which had recently been highly criticized for sloppy administration of grants and contributions. Rather than take the risk of dealing with a new organization, it made a financial contribution to Hay West's administration costs of $150,000 through the Canadian Federation of Humane Societies. This created considerably more work for Hay West and added $10,000 to the cost of administration.

The arrangement with CFHS was effective in issuing tax receipts but resulted in some suspicion in the farming community. Not everyone in the farming community is thrilled about the work of their local humane society. While farmers support the broad aims of humane societies, especially the proper treatment and care of animals, they sometimes run into conflicts when societies take very aggressive positions on what might be considered normal practice. Likewise, it might be that not all humane society volunteers are comfortable supporting a relief effort designed to fatten cattle for slaughter. While CFHS was eager to point out that there was nothing incompatible between their concerns for animal welfare and the practices of most Canadian farmers, there was always some background skepticism among farmers about a partnership with a humane society.

CFHS was very keen on getting involved in fundraising and seemed to want to raise its profile in the media. This was not the role that Hay West wanted for CFHS, which was strictly to issue tax receipts, pay the bills and fulfill statutory tax obligations. As a result, many conflicts arose between the Hay West board and CFHS, and relations were not always constructive and positive. Despite numerous efforts to strike a written agreement between Hay West and CFHS, none was forthcoming. Many frustrating and divisive meetings were held, and in the end most on the Hay West board concluded it would have been better to partner with a different charitable organization.

One farming organization that did greatly assist Hay West fundraising was the Agricultural Institute of Canada (AIC). The AIC is the national organization promoting the profession of agrology and the science of agriculture. More importantly, its executive director, Patty Townsend, assisted by another executive member, Jean Sullivan, was a spark plug of energy who generously applied her mastery of communications to the cause of Hay West. AIC, like CFHS, raised money on behalf of Hay West and issued tax receipts to donors.

Hay West volunteer and farm activist Patty Townsend enjoying a laugh with Willard McWilliams and Ottawa Mayor Bob Chiarelli.
Photo: Hay West volunteer.

In the end, it was important to the success of Hay West that it have organizational clarity. The process of incorporation forced the organization to establish roles and responsibilities that ultimately served the organization very well.

Notes

1 Bob Plamondon is also the author of this book.

The Politics of Hay West

Hay West was a community-driven initiative that supported nation building. It was also a media darling. These elements made it an attractive to governments, who ultimately wanted to be recognized as supportive.

Most farming leaders would have preferred the federal government to send billions of dollars directly to weary, drought-stricken farmers. But it was not that easy. Government already had an array of programs to help farmers: crop insurance, deferred savings accounts and emergency relief. From a policy perspective, the federal government wanted established programs to respond to the crisis. In the end, they hoped that what was already in place would, in time, constitute an adequate response to the drought.

"We monitored the drought very closely," said Agriculture Minister Lyle Vanclief. "We needed to have a clear idea what the draw was going to be on crop insurance. Because of the severity of the drought, we also wanted to expedite the delivery of cheques under existing programs as fast as we could."

Vanclief knows farming and farm programs. A farmer himself for over 25 years, he purchased crop insurance, experienced drought and faced the same risks and worry that Canadian farmers encounter each and every year. Perhaps as a result of his personal experience, Minister Vanclief takes a very business-oriented approach to farming. "When I thought the risk was manageable, I didn't buy crop insurance. But I certainly would have no one else to blame if there was a crop failure that I chose not to insure."

Prime Minister Chrétien addresses a Hay West rally in Smiths Falls, Ontario, with Cabinet Minister Don Boudria in the background.
Photo: Diana Murphy, Office of the Prime Minister.

Agriculture and Agri-Food Minister Lyle Vanclief talks to reporters before meeting with provincial and territorial agriculture ministers.
Photo: Agriculture and Agri-Food Canada.

The Agriculture Department tracked conditions in the West through the Prairie Farm Rehabilitation Administration (PFRA). The PFRA is an agency of Agriculture and Agri-Food Canada that works with prairie farmers to help them meet the challenges presented by a demanding climate and to ensure the sustainable use of the prairie's soil and water resources.

Despite the record drought conditions in certain parts of the West, at no time during the summer of 2002 did the Agriculture Minister or his department consider alternative policy responses to the situation. Indeed, as news reports of the drought became more numerous, the first response from the federal Department of Agriculture was to issue a press release in July 2002 that simply listed the various federal support programs that were available to farmers. While the Department of Agriculture was looking at ways to expedite payments to farmers suffering from the drought, there was no new policy initiative or funding to help farmers. However, the creation of Hay West gave the federal government another position from which it could be helpful.

"When my staff first told me about Hay West, I told them to do what they could to help," said Vanclief. That led to a number of supports for Hay West including staff resources to facilitate federal involvement, administrative funds to manage donations, a commitment to pay all costs related to fumigation and dollars for railcars.

Randy Fletcher, the minister's legislative assistant and political staffer for Ontario, was assigned virtually full-time to the Hay West file. Fletcher attended most Hay West meetings and kept in contact with the organizers on a routine basis. This included working weekends and even answering the odd 4:00 A.M. call, such as when he was asked if he would approve reimbursing the costs of portable toilets used at rail yards.

Leading the Hay West file in the Department of Agriculture and Agri-Food Canada was its Director General of Asset Management and Capital Planning, Pierre Corriveau, with the Director of Material Management, James McKendry, assisting him. On most days these civil servants tend to the finance, procurement and engineering needs of the department, which means they spend about $100 million each year on goods and services. They are also responsible for emergency services, which gave them lead responsibility during the Ice Storm, Y2K and the power failure in Southern Ontario in 2003. When the department looked to the people best suited to help Hay West, this emergency response team was the one they chose.

Corriveau's team provided support in a number of ways. First, they helped Hay West procure a government office equipped with computers and a toll-free line. These facilities, provided by Public Works Canada, were not otherwise in use at the time meaning the incremental cost was either nil or a very small amount.

The Government of Canada also provided $150,000 to Hay West to pay for various items including office staff, loading costs at the rail yard, administrative expenses and other related costs. For a fee of $10,000, the Canadian Federation of Humane Societies administered this fund. In a similar vein, Agriculture Canada also provided funds to help offset unloading costs in the West with a total of $225,000 going to the Saskatchewan Cattle Feeders Association and the Alberta 4-H.

The $150,000 contribution to office costs was extremely valuable to Hay West. "As we got to mid-August, friends were getting harder to find," remarked Wyatt McWilliams. "We had asked so much of the community and volunteers, and we couldn't keep asking for more. With the government money, we could at least help pay some of the expenses of the volunteers."

The more significant cost incurred by the federal government was for fumigation and railcars, which would eventually total $3.8 million. During the months of August through October, keeping track of these expenses was virtually a full-time job for McKendry. "We kept track of each shipment of hay. We needed to ensure that fumigation certificates and travel documents were in place and *needed to know* what financial exposure the government faced for the railcars," said McKendry. This was done in cooperation with Transport Canada.

The support of the Minister of Agriculture and the Prime Minister led to near-record response and delivery times for government support. It took only seven days from the day the government first indicated that administrative support would be available before a cheque for half the promised funds was delivered to Hay West's agent—dropped off at a Tim Horton's donut shop to speed the process.

It is noteworthy, however, that Deputy Minister Samy Watson did not ask the Agriculture Department's policy and operations group to take the lead or even be involved in Hay West. It seemed odd at first to Hay West that the group that designed farm income assistance programs was not directly involved in the relief effort. It was as if the department did not want existing program officers to be distracted by the Hay West relief effort. The Deputy Minister also insisted that the department's regular operations not be diminished as a result of Hay West. As a consequence, none of the federal government's contribution to Hay West came from Agriculture Canada's base budget; rather it came from "the center," namely the Treasury Board's reserve fund for contingencies. Securing the support of the Prime Minister's Office was critical in gaining access to the reserve fund.

Similarly, the Department of Agriculture did not seem to want to accept any additional obligations as a consequence of the drought in Western Canada and wanted existing programs to operate as intended. It is interesting that nowhere in the department's lexicon are the words *drought* or *disaster* defined. Nowhere in the policy framework does a new stream of money become available when climate conditions reach extreme levels.

The separation of government support for Hay West from Department of Agriculture programs was, in the end, perhaps not as curious as it first seemed. The Government of Canada was careful to separate its support for the Hay West relief effort from the direct financial contributions that would be made through the existing farm income support programs. This ensured that resources given to Hay West did not deplete funds allocated to existing farm income support programs. Yet, in the midst of the drought, no one from the PMO was asking whether the existing policy framework would ultimately provide an adequate response to the drought.

The low-profile approach taken by the Department of Agriculture seems consistent with Minister Vanclief's style. He does not seem to have a personality that publicly reaches out with emotion and sympathy to "feel the pain" of others when they are facing hard times. He is rather a logical man who holds that success is the result of hard work and intelligence and that farmers who had failed to prudently manage risk shouldn't expect much sympathy.

While Department of Agriculture officials facilitated the flow of money to Hay West, they did not want to take credit for their contributions. Indeed, government announcements for Hay West did not come from the Agriculture Department; they were on the letterhead of Minister of State Don Boudria. Under the heading "Government of Canada Pitches in on Hay West Campaign" Minister Boudria's August 1, 2002, press release stated: "When the Prime Minister learned about Hay West, he made it clear that he wanted the government to pitch in. I meet regularly with Hay West organizers, many of whom come from my riding. After consultations with government officials, we agreed on the kind of assistance from our government that will best help them meet the challenges of getting the hay to farmers who need it."[1]

In the statement, the government committed to covering the costs of the fumigation of donated hay, reimbursing some of the costs associated with loading the donated hay and providing Canadian Forces' logistical assistance in coordinating delivery and loading donated of hay at the railhead. "The Hay West campaign demonstrates the very best in the Canadian spirit—the desire to come to the aid of fellow citizens in times of trouble. I commend the farmers, volunteers and businesses who have pulled together to make the campaign possible. And I want to make special mention of the pledge by the CN Rail, CP Rail and Ottawa Central Railway to transport the hay free of charge,"[2] said Minister Boudria. Nowhere in the press release was the Department of Agriculture even mentioned.

General Manager Pierre Brodeur kept Minister Don Boudria, Randy Fletcher and PMO staffer Marjory Loveys informed of Hay West activity on a daily basis. They could see what was working well and what needed improvement. As the campaign progressed, the clear limiting factor was transportation resources.

If there was a Minister of Hay West it would have been the Hon. Don Boudria, shown here receiving an award from western farmers for his assistance to Hay West.
Photo: Office of Don Boudria.

Ontario and Quebec farmers were doing their part by donating hay, including increasing demands from many parts of Atlantic Canada to donate hay to the cause. The railways had contributed 187 railcars and corporations and others had paid for an additional 148 cars, but funds were drying up. Hay West couldn't go back to the railways to ask for more than they had given already. As the generosity of farmers grew, there was a very real prospect that mountains of hay would end up sitting at rail yards across Eastern Canada with no resources to move it west. There was a fear that the substantial toil of hundreds of generous Eastern farmers might end up going to waste.

Because of the widespread community support, not to mention the voluminous press reports, those representing the federal government on the Hay West file thought they could justify doing more. Hay West had become a nation-building operation that had the clear and strong support of farmers, corporations and individual Canadians. The federal government's proposal was to provide enough funds to match the number of railcars Hay West had mustered on its own. This meant donating 190 cars on top of the 187 that were previously given to match what the railways had provided.

"This was not a decision based on economics," said Minister Vanclief, "We wanted to help those who were trying to help others." In a somewhat ironic and humorous tone, Marjory Loveys remarked, "Finally, we had an issue where the economists did not rule." The media picked up on this issue and even began to look at Hay West with a critical eye. A lengthy CBC radio spot on August 23 reported on the economics of shipping hay east to west. One idea explored was to send Western beef east, where the cattle forage was plentiful, rather than shipping the hay out West. It was suggested that shipping the cattle would be cheaper than shipping the hay.

Economics would have dictated that all hay donated from Western Ontario should be shipped before allowing

Nova Scotia volunteers were proud to display their involvement with Hay West by making up signs on their own.
Photo: Hay West volunteer.

hay to move from the Maritimes. Yet the farmers of PEI, Nova Scotia and New Brunswick wanted to be part of Hay West—and they wanted to be a part of it now, not later if the supply dwindled in Ontario. Government funding made it possible for more farmers from more regions of the country to contribute. To emphasize the nation-building dimension of Hay West, Government of Canada trucks were used to haul hay across the Confederation Bridge from PEI to New Brunswick.

After all the work that Eastern farmers and others had put into Hay West, Don Boudria was infuriated when he read a newspaper column in which MP Kevin Sorenson criticized the federal government for its role. "Why undermine an effort to which people are giving their heart and soul? I told Sorenson that his words were discouraging to those in the East who were trying to help," Boudria said. His point was well taken. At no point did any federal official or politician take exception to the work of the Hay

Ray Dupuis of Midland Transport heads toward the Confederation Bridge en route to Moncton with a delivery of hay.
Photo: Constituency office of Wayne Easter, MP for Malpeque.

West campaign. However, for Western MPs like Sorenson, it was almost impossible to help Hay West without claiming that what was really needed was hundreds of millions of dollars of additional federal government assistance. What was being spent on drought relief by the federal government through existing programs, and through Hay West, was, in their opinion, simply not enough.

With all the momentum growing for Hay West across the country, it was perhaps natural that staff from the various federal government departments should want to witness the initiative in action. So it was that PMO staffer Marjory Loveys took the opportunity one weekend to visit the Hay West loading site in Ottawa with her husband. It was when she was meeting with Pierre Brodeur that the idea came up of bringing the Prime Minister to a loading site.

The next day, Loveys discussed the issue with Don Boudria, who immediately took it to the Prime Minister. Prime Minister Chrétien liked what Hay West was doing and gave his blessing for an event. Planning got into full swing with PMO officials in communications taking the lead.

The loading in Ottawa was almost complete, so an alternate sight was required. Smiths Falls, a town of about 9,000 people located about 75 kilometers west of Ottawa, was selected. It was an ideal site because all freight trains operating between Eastern and Western Canada pass through the town. As it turned out, more hay was loaded at Smiths Falls than at any other location.

The day of the visit was August 7. Don Boudria drove out to the event with Prime Minister Chrétien, which gave him ample opportunity to talk about the initiative and the people involved.

Boudria kicked off the official ceremony, noting that what had begun only three weeks ago from a simple phone call had turned into a national initiative that had brought together the efforts of countless volunteers across Canada. He admitted that when Councillor Phil McNeely approached him about shipping hay across the second largest country on the face of the earth, it had not appeared to be a realistic idea. He recalled the Ice Storm of 1998 and how people from across the country had chipped in to help and explained how he thought it was worth exploring how the generosity might be returned. Mr. Boudria reminded those in attendance that Canada was built on railways and that this tradition continued with Hay West.

The Prime Minister went to the podium. His unedited remarks follow:

"Thank you, Don. Your Worship, Mayor Dennis Staples, Phil McNeely and Bob Kilgour, my good friend from Cornwall and dear friends, ladies and gentlemen. One of the great traditions of Canada is that we help each other in times of trouble. Our sense of being family bridges the vast distances of our country. When hardship hits, our instinctive reaction is to reach out and to help.

"Our instinct is to do what is possible to help others. During the terrible drought of the 1930s, the farmers of the Atlantic sent food to the people of the West. During the ice storm of 1998, Western Canadians sent relief to the people of Ontario and Quebec. Hay West is about continuing that great Canadian tradition of sharing and caring. Farmers in Eastern Ontario have seen the suffering of Western farmers and livestock in the worse drought ever to hit Western Canada. Led by Wyatt and Willard McWilliams, they have done something about it.

"They wanted to share their bounty; friends and neighbors eagerly lent a hand. CN, CP and the Ottawa Central Railroad have provided free transport. Many local businesses have donated equipment, Councillor Phil McNeely has dedicated his office and staff to that effort, and our government has pitched in too under the direction of our very good friend Don Boudria to help make sure the hay can get to where it's needed and as fast as possible.

"Everyone who has been asked to help has answered the call very quickly, and we were all moved by the pictures of the first shipment of hay when it arrived out West. By the emotion of the farmers and the sense of appreciation, of course, no amount of generosity will relieve all the suffering; only a steady rain will do that. Governments, as always, will be there to provide farmers with disaster assistance. But Hay West is about responding in a much more direct and immediate way. It is farmer to farmer; it is family to family, community to community, Canadian to Canadian. That is the story of Hay West, and that is the story of this great country, Canada. Thank you very much."[3]

At the conclusion of the ceremony Wyatt McWilliams presented the Prime Minister with a Hay West hat.

The PMO was very happy with the Smiths Falls event, which was carried live on national television. This is the kind of treatment one might expect for a federal budget or the launch of a space shuttle; yet national television thought the nation wanted to see the Prime Minister don a Hay West cap.

Everyone from the PMO who attended remarked that what was happening at the Smiths Falls rail yards was operationally impressive. "Sometimes when you make a decision to support an initiative, all you really see is a flow of paper, usually in the form of a cheque to another government that ultimately spends the money," said Marjory Loveys. "When we went to Smiths Falls, we could see very tangibly what we were supporting. This was a huge physical undertaking. It was very impressive, almost stunning."

That didn't stop some newspaper columnists from criticizing the Prime Minister for cozying up to the highly publicized and well-meaning Hay West initiative. "You are going to be criticized no matter what," said Loveys. "We

Prime Minister Chrétien delivering remarks about Hay West at the Smiths Falls rail yard, aired live on national television on CBC Newsworld.
Photo Diana Murphy, Office of the Prime Minister.

Wyatt McWilliams gives Prime Minister Chrétien a Hay West hat.
Photo Diana Murphy, Office of the Prime Minister.

were asked by Hay West to attend, and the Prime Minister wanted to show his support for some incredibly good works. It was as simple as that."

The Prime Minister's involvement did not sit well with some Canadians. They wanted the government to do much more to help, as a letter to the *Ottawa Citizen* reflected:

"It was disheartening to see Prime Minister Jean Chrétien literally climbing onto the wagon with his crisp new 'Hay West' cap and talking about the virtues of 'caring and sharing.' Where is the leadership and the take-charge approach?

"The drought on the prairies is a national disaster, not a provincial or regional problem. As a nation, we have an obligation to protect and foster our national food supply. We are not a nation from sea to sea or a confederation if we cannot help our Western neighbors.

"The only level of government that has the capability to deal with such a transprovincial border calamity is the federal government. It has the emergency measures organizational structure and our taxpayer resources to do it.

"It should not be up to some local heroes such as the McWilliams family in Navan, who started the relief effort.

"Mr. Chrétien must activate the levers of the federal government to move hay rapidly from the shores of the Atlantic across Canada to Alberta.

"Use the budget surpluses that Paul Martin squirreled away into holding accounts during his tenure at Finance. Otherwise, the train is leaving the station, and Mr. Chrétien has again missed the occasion to initiate but prefers to jump on the hay wagon."

–Paul Marcinov

Ottawa, Ontario[4]

One editorial suggested that Eastern farmers would have done more good by putting pressure on federal politicians to deliver billions in financial relief, rather than shipping relatively small amounts of hay out West. "Since they are down East, close to the seat of power, they should have, on behalf of Western farmers, taken their 1,000 tonnes of hay and stacked it on the lawn in front of the House of Commons. They should have told Jean Chrétien to deal with the unprecedented problem in Western Canada—a problem that could hinder the West's economic development for years."[5] Whatever the editorialist's intentions, he clearly did not understand the McWilliams' style and motives. They are not protestors by nature. To them, Hay West was not about politics. They just wanted to get things done—and done quickly.

While the sense of Western alienation was undoubtedly alleviated to a degree by the generosity of farmers from the East, federal government support for Hay West did not translate into a corresponding appreciation for the national government. A *Calgary Herald*–Global on-line poll asked, "Who is helping drought-stricken farmers the most?" Sixty-one percent of Canadians responded that Hay West led the way. Eighteen percent felt that Alberta was doing the most, while 16 percent thought the rail companies were helping the most. Only 5 percent of Canadians believed that the federal government had taken the lead in disaster relief.[6]

Kevin Sorenson, MP for Crowfoot Alberta, implored Agriculture Minister Lyle Vanclief to visit the drought-stricken areas. Sorenson remembered Vanclief's reply. "Kevin, I have been a farmer for 25 years. I think I know what a drought looks like." When Sorenson told the minister of the absolute devastation, the parched soil and the infestation of grasshoppers, he was told, "Kevin, you make this sound like a plague of biblical proportions." Sorenson had the sense that the minister was being insensitive.

Ultimately, following public pressure stirred by the media, Minister Vanclief made the trip west and visited some farms around Leduc, Alberta, near the Edmonton airport. According to Sorenson, this area would not have been included in a list of fields that were hardest hit. Vanclief replied, "I went exactly where they asked me to go."

After touring farms around Leduc, Vanclief remarked, "Folks, I have to tell you I kind of get goose bumps when we see these types of things that show how Canada can really work and how Canada does work."[7]

Following the visit, Premier Ralph Klein offered the minister a backhanded compliment: "I have to commend Mr. Vanclief for coming out here to see firsthand the severity of the situation. But having said that, it's unfortunate that it took him so long." The Minister replied, "I'm on the ground today. I wasn't physically here [earlier], but I'm certainly there doing the job putting the programs together and seeking the resources."[8]

Some argue that the federal response to the drought disaster of 2002 compares poorly with how it responded to other disasters, such as the Ice Storm. In this regard, Myron Thompson, MP for Wildrose Alberta, rose the House of Commons on December 10, 2002, to say:

"When the drought was first announced and things began to happen, through generosity, the great people from Ontario and other parts of the country came to the aid of farmers, farmer to farmer. The government did absolutely nothing in terms of that disaster. Yet with other disasters, it rose to the occasion. It helped with the floods of Quebec. We know how well we did in responding to the Ice Storm. There has been no response at all to the drought, and it looks like we are on our way to another year of serious drought, yet it is not being talked about."[9]

In a year-end interview with Minister Vanclief, Southam News looked back at the federal response to the drought of 2002. "No response is flawless," Vanclief said. "When there are circumstances like that, I think it's only human nature that people ask the questions, 'Well, why didn't you do more and why didn't you do it sooner?'"[10]

The article noted that Prime Minister Jean Chrétien's political minister for Saskatchewan, Ralph Goodale, acknowledged that the Liberal government "could have moved faster in assuring Western farmers it was responding to the drought crisis."[11]

Vanclief defended the government by pointing to the $3.8 million Ottawa contributed to help Hay West. "If the Federal government hadn't paid for all the fumigation of the hay from Eastern Canada, the product couldn't have gone. We have to recognize that in a country this size, there are always areas every year that are too hot or too cold, too wet or too dry, and that we do have a number of programs in place."[12]

Hay West board member and beef farmer Lloyd Craig remembered when the government acted swiftly and decisively to help farmers in crisis. "In the summer of 1963," he recalled, "Eastern Ontario was in drought, and we had to scour the province and elsewhere to find hay. Right off the bat, the government set up a program that subsidized the cost of hay to normal prices. There was a sense back then that the government was on the side of farmers. In 2002 the government did very little to help Western farmers." Craig believes that farmers themselves have "picked up the slack" for government inaction. "In 1963 there was no donated hay. With Hay West, the entire farming community stepped up to the plate. We all know it is a matter of survival."

While there were many in the West calling for the federal government to respond with billions in direct aid to farmers, as far as the Hay West board of directors was concerned, the federal government gave them everything they asked for. Hay West was never intended to be a government initiative. Yet, governments still stepped up and quickly made important and timely contributions to complement what farmers, corporations and individual Canadians were giving. The government of Alberta made a key contribution, and federal ministers, MPs and civil servants responded enthusiastically and cooperatively to Hay West. Nevertheless, it is clear that Western farmers and many Canadians would have preferred much more.

NOTES

1 Boudria, Don. Press release. Government of Canada, Minister of State, 1 August 2002.

2 Ibid.

3 Chrétien, Hon. Jean. Speech. Smith Falls, Ontario, 7 August 2002.

4 Marcinov, Paul. Letter to the editor. *Ottawa Citizen* 16 August 2004, sec. A: 13.

5 Belugessner, Paul, "The wrong things for the right reasons." *Swan Valley Star and Times* 20 August 2002, sec. A: 10.

6 "Question of the Day." *Calgary Herald* 20 August 2002, sec. A: 15.

7 Bell, Rick. "Vanclief MIA: Agriculture minister absent during farmers' time of need." *The Calgary Sun* 18 August 2002, sec. A: 5

8 Ibid.

9 Thompson, Myron. *Hansard*, 37th parliament, 2nd session, edited. Number 002, Government of Canada, 10 December 2002.

10 Mofina, Rick. "Vanclief defends Liberal government aid for Western farmers." *Port Hope Evening Guide* 2 January 2003, sec. A: 12

11 Ibid.

12 Ibid.

Hay West in Parliament

Hay West brought attention to the plight of Western farmers, which prompted an Emergency Debate in the House of Commons.

Photo: Corel.

The Parliament of Canada was not in session when Hay West operations were in full swing throughout the summer and early autumn. However, before the House rose for the summer recess on June 21, Alberta MP Kevin Sorenson alerted members to the early indications of a drought in the West. "Although I am looking forward to the next few months in my riding," he said before the House, "I dread witnessing the despair and loss of hope, given the serious drought in my constituency. Provost, Consort, Wainwright, Camrose, Stettler, Hanna, Drumheller and Oyen, as well as other parts of Central Alberta, have had no rain, prompting many constituents like Kurt and Lynn Cole to write. They said: 'Depression is written on people's faces as they are forced to sell their cattle and as they consider what they are going to do about their land that is drying and blowing away. . . . Intelligent, hard working people simply cannot compete. . . . There just is no release. As we sit and listen to you guys in parliament . . . our dear neighbor has taken his cattle [that have] been in his family for two generations to market.' For the sake of my constituents and all Canadian farmers," Sorenson continued, "I beg the government to do something to restore hope and to address this serious and devastating situation. The government should do more than flip a coin with the hopes of farmers: heads, government wins; tails, farmers lose."[1]

With that the House adjourned for the summer and did not reconvene until September 30, when Hay West operations had begun to taper off. The speech from the throne, which sets forth the government's priorities for the coming session of parliament, made no reference to the drought in Western Canada. However, as soon as the business of parliament was open to members on both sides of the House, the activities of Hay West were repeatedly mentioned in debate.

On the first day of parliamentary business on October 1, 2002, Carol Skelton, MP for Saskatoon–Rosetown–Biggar, rose to ask about the crisis in Western agriculture. "Yesterday's throne speech talked about putting Canadian families and children first," she said. "I have news for the Liberals: farm families include children. Yet the throne speech, in its 15 seconds about agriculture, failed to address the agriculture crisis. Why are the Liberals ignoring the needs of farm families at a time when severe drought and massive agriculture subsidies in the U.S. farm bill threaten the very existence of the Canadian family farm?"[2]

In his reply, Minister of Agriculture and Agri-Food Lyle Vanclief insisted that the government had made substantial investments in support for farmers to help them mitigate all problems, weather included. "On June 20 of this year," he reminded the House, "the Prime Minister and I announced the biggest farm support package in many years for Canadian farmers, with a number of elements, including risk management. Since that time, we also have put in place . . . $600 million to assist Canadian farm families for the various types of threats that they have been undergoing in the last year. . . . No government has come forward in recent years with as much support to Canadian farm families and Canadian farmers as this government."[3]

The day following, Mrs. Skelton again rose in the House, this time to give tribute to the work of Hay West:

"Mr. Speaker, for the second year in a row, farm families on the prairies have watched their crops and pastures wither and the dust fly as drought continues to grip most of Canada's grainbelt.

"When a group of our farming neighbors in the Eastern provinces heard about the drought conditions on the prairies, they decided to do what they could to help, and the Hay West campaign was born. There are many people who deserve thanks for their donations to this campaign, but the organizers of the Hay West Initiative deserve special recognition.

"I have had the pleasure of meeting two of the people behind the Hay West campaign, Willard McWilliams and Cumberland Councillor Phil McNeely, who have given hours of their own time and resources to coordinate the donations of thousands of tonnes of hay to Western farmers. They have taken on a huge job out of their own goodwill and through the kindness of their hearts.

"On behalf of the constituents of Saskatoon–Rosetown–Biggar, and indeed all the recipients of the much-needed hay, I want to congratulate the people who have led the Hay West campaign and extend a huge, heartfelt thanks."[4]

In rare circumstances, a Member of Parliament can request that the speaker grant permission to conduct an emergency debate, something Joe Clark, MP for Calgary Centre, did on October 4 in response the drought.

"The 2002 crop year will be remembered as one of the worst growing seasons for Western Canada," his speech began. "Many producers believe that conditions were the driest ever experienced in the West. The report shows that wheat production is expected to decline to the lowest level in 28 years.

"This past summer the whole country saw nightly news stories about efforts to save cattle herds in areas of severe drought," Clark continued. "Canadian farmers in central and Eastern Canada responded with the Hay West program and, belatedly, the federal government came on board to fund some railcars for the donations of hay. That was a minimal response. The federal government knew last spring that another drought was imminent, and yet no planning was done to put in place a disaster relief fund to help those farmers. . . .

"The throne speech made only the briefest mention of agriculture, and nothing was said about the desperate situation of farmers suffering from drought. The program announced earlier in the year is simply not adequate.

"We need a full discussion on ways to make government programs more responsive to the perils that face farming today. Agriculture is in a crisis which needs to be fully debated in an emergency debate in the House as soon as possible," [5] Clark concluded.

The Speaker of the House granted Clark's request and ordered the debate for October 7. As expected, the debate was combative and ran nearly four hours, during which the opposition praised the Hay West initiative and criticized the government response as too little too late. Opposition members challenged the government to create a permanent and appropriately funded disaster relief program for agriculture. The government countered that it had substantially increased its financial support for farmers and that funds would be delivered in short order. Almost everyone who spoke made glowing remarks about Hay West.

Joe Clark commended the "farmers in Ontario, Quebec and Atlantic Canada . . . for their initiative and their generosity." [6] Rick Borotsik, MP for Brandon–Souris, congratulated farmers for stepping forward to help other farmers in need, but he reminded the House that "less than 1 percent of the problem is being repaired by Hay West. . . . The major reason for this debate is so we can profile this and tell Canadians that the problem has not been fixed. The $600 million is not even a start to fixing the problem." [7]

Minister Vanclief responded: "I want to thank the volunteers who instigated the Hay West program. I get a little upset when people say that it was not meaningful. It was certainly meaningful to those who received hay. Everybody did not receive hay. The federal government rented 377 cars and paid for the fumigation of the hay. This was a project and a result that showed how Canada can and really does work. Individual hay producers in this case, as well as individuals who wanted to help, gave money from their own pockets. There were corporate donations as well to give some relief to producers in Western Canada who were suffering from drought." [8]

Stephen Harper, MP for Calgary Southwest and Leader of the Opposition, said, "The Hay West Initiative from many parts of Eastern Canada was a tremendous act of Canadians caring for other Canadians. It was genuinely appreciated in Western Canada. Even if ultimately the amounts of hay are small in terms of the total problem, it really does go to show that farm families are a very special breed of Canadian." But he reminded the House of the human dimension to the drought crisis when he recounted how prairie MPs "have been overwhelmed . . . by the emotional stories of worry, anxiety, anger, sadness and despair that they have found on the prairies." [9]

Carol Skelton, MP for Saskatoon–Rosetown–Biggar, echoed Harper's claims. "My office in Saskatoon took over 4,000 calls for hay when the Hay West campaign was born," she stated. "People phoned, faxed, cried on the telephone, told terrible stories of hardship and pleaded for hay and help.

"I want to thank from the bottom of my heart the people of Eastern Canada who gave so much to Western Canada. We heard tonight that it was just a pittance, but those bales and those railcars that came to Western Canada gave our people hope. There was a message of sincere sympathy from Eastern producers saying that we do care. I wish the Government of Canada cared as much for our producers as the people in Eastern Canada did.

"On July 27 I received a letter that was addressed to the Prime Minister, the Minister of Agriculture and the Minister of Rural Development in Canada. It reads: 'Sir, I write this letter with much sadness and a very heavy heart. A short time ago a neighbor of mine committed suicide because of depression, a condition caused in large measure by frustration and hopelessness due to very poor grain, oilseed, specialty crop prices and declining livestock prices, drought and the added threat of a heavy grasshopper infestation. I spoke with him a few days before his death at which time he could see no way out of his situation because of huge input costs and a serious shortfall in income.'

"Last week we read in the Saskatoon *StarPhoenix* obituary column of a young farm lady who committed suicide also from depression."[10]

Dick Proctor, MP for Palliser, challenged the House to measure the federal government's response to the drought in the context of its response to previous natural disasters. "Six of the last nine emergency debates since 1997 have been on agriculture," he reminded. "Do members know that an emergency debate that we did not have was one after the Ice Storm in 1997–98? Why? Because the government moved and moved quickly to assist Ontario and Quebec farmers. That is not lost on people in Western Canada. . . . As a result of the government inaction, Canadian farmers from Eastern Ontario, Quebec and the Maritimes initiated a Hay West campaign to assist their Western counterparts. It was a great initiative in nation building, as has been pointed out by virtually all the previous speakers. . . .

"However . . . [f]or all the ballyhoo that the Hay West campaign generated this summer, it amounted to less than 1 percent of the hay that is required to feed the livestock this winter. Whoever said it was like offering two pizzas to a city on the verge of starvation put it in the proper context, but it did serve the public relations purpose: a photo op of a government and a Prime Minister who really, really care. It had nothing to do with rolling up their sleeves and doing the right thing. Rather, it was to make the federal government look good in Ontario and elsewhere and to give the impression that the feed problem in Western Canada had been solved. Hay West was a great initiative by some well-meaning and caring folks who gave hay, hard work and a lot of time and effort, and a cynical government tried to capitalize on that initiative."[11]

David Anderson, MP for Cypress Hills–Grasslands, stated that "if it had not been for . . . the generosity of the individuals in Ontario, probably nothing would have happened to help out those [Western] farmers because the government certainly was not responsive to them."[12] Rob Merrifield, MP for Yellowhead, carried the argument further, maintaining that "It was very late in the game when the government finally decided almost out of embarrassment that it would fork over a few measly dollars (I think it was $3.8 million) to send 377 loads of hay to Western Canada, which was very much appreciated." His address echoed the concerns of many opposition MPs when he concluded: "The frustrating thing is that this needs to be levered into action by a government that has the dollars to be able to really deal with the problem. The amount of hay on those trains is enough to be goodwill and is very much appreciated, but it is certainly not enough to address the problem in Western Canada."[13]

It was left to Peter MacKay, MP for Pictou–Antigonish–Guysborough, to sum up most eloquently how Canadians felt about Hay West and how Canadians had every right to look to their federal government to enlarge the generous gesture made by Eastern farmers:

"The Hay West program was a wonderful effort, again a truly pan-Canadian effort that saw farmers coming together from different parts of the country to help other farmers. It was done purely out of the goodness of their hearts and there is nothing that rekindles people's faith in the human spirit more than gratuitous acts of kindness. That is what the Hay West program was all about. I am proud that Nova Scotia took part in that.

"These types of reciprocal arrangements and acts of kindness have been there for a long time. In the East, during the hungry thirties, fish, food and clothing were sent from Eastern provinces to the West. I am sure that it would be reciprocated.

"I know that there is a great empathy that exists in regions like ours in Atlantic Canada. We have been through the collapse of the fishery. We understand hard times.

"This approach that has been taken to reach out to help people in need is one that truly has to be encouraged and applauded at times. Caring, compassionate people span all politics and regions. It is something that Canadians do and do well. We take care of our own. We are not, unfortunately, able to say that at this point in time because we are not doing enough to help the agriculture industry."[14]

All parliamentarians joined to congratulate Wyatt and Willard McWilliams' initiative when the two were introduced to the House of Commons from the gallery on November 6 by John Harvard, MP for Charleswood–St. James–Assiniboia:

"Mr. Speaker, we have in Ottawa today two extraordinary gentlemen from Navan, Ontario, Willard and Wyatt McWilliams.

"On July 17 last summer, the father and son farming duo were discussing the terrible situation of drought stricken farmers in Western Canada. After consulting their MP, who happens to be our esteemed House Leader, the Hay West Initiative was born. Less than four months later, 1,800 farmers in Ontario, Quebec, New Brunswick and Nova Scotia had pledged more than 30,000 tonnes of hay that was shipped to Alberta and Saskatchewan by over 700 railcars and 160 trucks. Canadian citizens and corporate Canada donated farm equipment, thousands of volunteer hours and over $1 million. In total, about 1,000 farming families in Alberta and Saskatchewan received the much-needed hay thanks to Willard and Wyatt McWilliams.

"As chair of the Western Liberal caucus, I wish to express my appreciation as well as extend my congratulations to the McWilliams for their ability to show Canadians how things are done in Canada when people are in need."[15]

The recognition and tribute given to Hay West in the Parliament of Canada by politicians from every political stripe speaks to what Hay West accomplished by all Canadians. Whatever the debate within the House of Commons about the government's response to the plight of Western farmers, no one doubted that Willard and Wyatt McWilliams, and all those involved with Hay West, had given their all.

Notes

1 Sorenson, Kevin. *Hansard*, 37th parliament, 1st session, edited, Government of Canada, 14 June 2002.

2 Skelton, Carol. *Hansard*, 37th parliament, 2nd session, edited, number 002, Government of Canada, 1 October 2002.

3 Vanclief, Lyle. *Hansard*, 37th parliament, 2nd session, edited, number 002, Government of Canada, 1 October 2002.

4 Skelton, Carol *Hansard*, 37th parliament, 2nd session, edited, number 002, Government of Canada, 2 October 2002.

5 Clark, Joe. *Hansard*, 37th parliament, 2nd session, edited, number 002, Government of Canada, 4 October 2002.

6 Clark, Joe. *Hansard*, 37th parliament, 2nd session, edited, number 002, Government of Canada, 7 October 2002.

7 Borotsik, Rick. *Hansard*, 37th parliament, 2nd session, edited, number 002, Government of Canada, 7 October 2002.

8 Vanclief, Lyle. *Hansard*, 37th parliament, 2nd session, edited, number 002, Government of Canada, 7 October 2002.

9 Harper, Stephen. *Hansard*, 37th parliament, 2nd session, edited, number 002, Government of Canada, 7 October 2002.

10 Skelton, Carol. *Hansard*, 37th parliament, 2nd session, edited, number 002, Government of Canada, 7 October 2002.

11 Proctor, Dick. *Hansard*, 37th parliament, 2nd session, edited, number 002, Government of Canada, 7 October 2002.

12 Anderson, David. *Hansard*, 37th parliament, 2nd session, edited, number 002, Government of Canada, 7 October 2002.

13 Merrifield, Rob. *Hansard*, 37th parliament, 2nd session, edited, number 002, Government of Canada, 7 October 2002.

14 MacKay, Peter. *Hansard*, 37th parliament, 2nd session, edited, number 002, Government of Canada, 7 October 2002.

15 Harvard, John *Hansard*, 37th parliament, 2nd session, edited, number 002, Government of Canada, 6 November 2002.

To account for how much money was spent on Hay — the check reads:

Dec. 18   20__

Pay to the Order of **Hay West**

Finances

Five Thousand Dollars $ **5,000**.00

CCEA ◆ AECC

Wyatt and Willard McWilliams receiving a symbolic cheque from Jack Graham of the Central Canada Exhibition at Ottawa City Hall on December 18, 2002, to the applause of Ottawa mayor Bob Chiarelli. The Exhibition has roots in the agricultural community. Photo: Jeffrey, City of Ottawa.

To account for how much money was spent on Hay West one must look in a number of places. First the Government of Canada spent about $3.8 million, most of which was used to pay for 376 railcars and for fumigation. Second, the railways donated almost 200 railcars while other corporations kicked in enough money to pay for an additional 135 railcars. Third, local communities raised the funds they needed to cover expenses at remote loading sites, usually by hosting barbecues and other social functions. Finally, $1.3 million were donated by concerned Canadians directly to Hay West.

Of the funds raised for Hay West, governments contributed $350,000; corporations, $420,000; and individuals or community groups, $525,000. Money was raised and spent either directly by Hay West or indirectly through its partners, the Agricultural Institute of Canada and the Canadian Federation of Humane Societies.

Crown corporations gave generously. Farm Credit Canada made a $50,000 contribution. Les Rankin, Vice-President, Marketing and Portfolio Management, said, "No one company or organization can change the situation, but working together with Hay West, we can lend our support to these farmers." Another crown corporation, Canada Mortgage and Housing Corporation, gave $11,000 to the relief effort.

On the corporate side, the Canadian Association of Petroleum Producers spearheaded an effort that resulted in contributions from its members totaling over $200,000.

Among these, Imperial Oil donated $25,000; Petro-Canada, $25,000; and Devon Canada, $20,000. Shell Oil contributed 40,000 liters of fuel to be used in both Eastern and Western Canada. "Farmers across Canada are Shell's customers and our neighbors," said Tim Faithfull, President and Chief Executive Officer of Shell Canada. "We feel it is important to do our part."

Other major corporations gave generously to Hay West. Power Corporation contributed $30,000. Pfizer, best known as a supplier of pharmaceuticals for humans but also offering products for the agricultural sector, donated $35,000. "These are tough times for the people and their livestock," said Andrew Moore, Director, Pfizer Animal Health Group. "We can't make it rain, stop the heartache producers are suffering or make up for what they have already lost. What we can do is pitch in and try to ease some of the financial pressure of getting hay to where it is needed most."

Everyone knows the connection between barley and beer. So it made sense for Molson to belly-up with some cash and railcars for Hay West. Molson additionally provided trucks to pick up 700 donated hay bales within the Halton, Peel, Dufferin and Wellington communities and deliver them for loading at the rail depot in Snelgrove, Ontario. Once the hay arrived in Killam, Alberta, additional Molson transports delivered the hay directly to drought-stricken farmers in the region. "We quickly realized that many of the resources that the relief effort lacks are right at our finger tips," explained Michael Downey, President, Ontario and West Divisions, Molson Canada. Molson drivers also contributed their time. "The union employees at Molson have been moved by this issue to the point which they have offered their personal commitment and are donating their time to the relief effort," said Benny

Molson provided money, trucking and logistical support for Hay West.
Photo: Hay West volunteer.

McAllister, President, Local 309, Brewery General and Professional Workers Union, Molson Canada.

Montana's Cookhouse restaurants helped to raise profile and money for Hay West by hosting an event for volunteers and workers at one of its Ottawa locations. Almost $10,000 was raised.

A collection taken at an Ottawa Renegades football game generated over $9,000; the team itself gave another $2,500 from ticket sales. The Central Canada Exhibition in Ottawa contributed $5,000.

Various community groups organized events to help Hay West, such as the Villeneuve Memorial Golf Tournament in Maxville, Ontario, which contributed $4,000. The Brockville District #1 Snowmobile Club gave $3,100; Northumberland Federation of Agriculture contributed $1,300; the Rotary Club of Ottawa chipped in $500. Some communities were so successful at fundraising to cover local expenses that they ended up with surpluses,

generous gift was the result of a single five-minute phone call. The donor wanted no fanfare and recognition; in fact, the donor wished to remain anonymous. Others did not have much to give, but they gave anyway.

Often it was the small donations that brought a lump to the throat of Hay West staff. These frequently arrived with letters such as the one written by Ron and Wilda Aspeck: "I grew up on a small farm East of Rockland, Ontario. I know how we depended on the weather for a good crop. My husband and I live on our old age pension and CPP, and we can spare $10. . . . We just wanted to do our part and pray for better weather and no grasshoppers." Mrs. Muriel Fitzgerald of Almonte Ontario wrote: "Enclosed is a small donation toward shipping the hay out West to help farmers cope with the terrible hardship they are having. This donation is out of my Old Age Security. I am not a farmer, nor do I come from a farming family, but I did live through the great depression and know what it means to need help."

The Government of Canada direct contribution of $150,000 to Hay West was used exclusively for loading hay, office staff, office expenses, insurance and the Canadian Federation of Humane Societies administration fee. This was an important contribution since Hay West could then spend every penny of corporate and private donations on getting hay out West.

The Province of Alberta contributed $200,000 to pay the cost of cutting and baling hay bound for Alberta. The administration of this fund was as simple and efficient as one could imagine. Alberta concluded they were dealing with honest and thrifty farmers who could be trusted with the hard-earned taxpayer dollars from the citizens of Alberta.

About half of the $1.3 million given to Hay West was spent on trucking. Other significant areas of costs were for

which were handed over for deposit to the Hay West bank account. For example, the Hay West fund from Chateauguay, Quebec, gave $4,000 to Hay West.

Almost from the moment word of Hay West hit the media, calls began coming in from individuals with offers of cash. Of note, one donor gave $200,000. This extremely

sands of hours given by some 1,600 volunteers and of course the donated hay, which, at market prices at the time, had a value of around $6 million. Beyond the hay, farmers and others donated their time and equipment for loading Hay in the East and unloading it in the West, for food and drink for volunteers at the rail yards and for the trucking of hay to the rail yards. Some volunteers' commitment was quite extraordinary, like the example Jack Durant, who trucked a total of 66 tractor-trailer loads of hay in Eastern Ontario.

Hay being unloaded at the Wainwright, Alberta, distribution center. Farm implement dealers like Tri-Ag and Wilmar implements donated equipment and staff to get the feed to farms quickly.
Photo: Kelly Clemmer, *The Wainwright Review.*

the cutting and transport of hay, staff and office expenses, and the fee paid to the Canadian Federation of Humane Societies for administrative services.

The Hay West board of directors kept a firm hand on the financial tiller of the organization, requiring detailed reports on a weekly basis. It was critical that budgets be kept up to date to ensure the initiative did not run a deficit and that all funds could be efficiently and promptly used.

At the end of the campaign board members were pleased to have a surplus of $200,000, which they divvied up among organizations in Western Canada supporting drought-stricken farmers. They were: Alberta 4-H; Saskatchewan 4-H; the Saskatchewan Cattle Feeders Association; and, Say Hay (an organization formed specifically to help Alberta farmers cope with the 2002 drought).

The nonfinancial donations given to the Hay West project were most important of all. These include many thou-

Hay Economics

While Hay West started off as a rail operation, the economics showed there was also a place for trucking.
Photo: Hay West volunteer.

When the hay was on the rails, and the nation voiced its admiration for what was being accomplished so quickly, questions were being asked about the economics of transporting such a heavy, bulky commodity over 4,000 kilometers by train and truck.

Perhaps the most vocal public critic of the economics of Hay West was Saskatchewan Liberal Senator Herb Sparrow. In a widely circulated news story, the senator criticized his own government for what he says was a "political hoax at the expense of needy farmers."[1] He argued that the government's involvement in Hay West was a waste of money that was being used to bolster the government's profile in agriculture. "My position," said Senator Sparrow, "is that the government should be spending the money more wisely on assistance to the agricultural producer in Saskatchewan"[2]

Sparrow, who himself farms grain in North Battleford, Saskatchewan, suggested that shipments from Hay West cost about $280 per ton, while the same amount of hay could be purchased locally for around $125 per ton. He called the differential "government waste." He went on to blame the federal government for "not understanding the problem that exists in the first place, not making an effort to search out the best approach to assist the agricultural producer, particularly those in the cattle industry, and probably doing it to get political kudos in Eastern Canada. It's indicated to the Easterners that this has solved the problem of feed shortage in Saskatchewan, and it hasn't done so. I don't want to take away the attitude that the

Ontario farmer is being generous in his offering, but in turn no one has explained to them what the ultimate cost is when it gets out here."[3]

Hay West sought to set the record straight in an open letter to the *Globe and Mail* of October 7, 2002:

Dear Mr. MacGregor:

I write with regard to your October 7 article entitled "Ottawa Made Hay out of Bailout: Senator" in which you quote Saskatchewan Senator Herb Sparrow's impressions of the value of the Hay West Initiative. It is hard to express the disappointment, concern and frustration that the Hay West organizers felt on reading this article and the claims made by the Honorable Senator regarding the efforts of Hay West.

Since Hay West did not have the opportunity to contribute the facts to the original story, we find it necessary to present them in this letter. Contrary to the quotes in the article, Hay West was not "perpetuated by the federal government." Hay West began as a project of Ontario farmers who wanted to help. Many of these farmers had benefited from the good will of Western farmers when they received donated generators, labor, materials and financial assistance to rebuild after the disastrous Ice Storm of 1998. They saw the devastation being wrought upon Alberta and Saskatchewan farmers by this drought, and they knew it was their turn to help. Their answer was to share the bountiful harvest of hay in the East with the drought-stricken areas of the West. It was only after these producers began to send hay West with volunteer labor and donated funds that the government decided to provide much-appreciated, but modest, assistance.

First fact: This project to help Western producers is built on donations and volunteers. More than 1,600 farmers have pledged almost 30,000 tonnes of hay to Hay West. For the most part, the hay has been cut, raked, baled, stacked, loaded, transported to rail yards and unloaded by volunteers. Equipment, fuel, baling inputs and time have been generously donated by rural citizens and their communities, and by corporate Canada. Canadians from across the country have made very generous financial donations to help move the donated hay west.

Second fact: The generosity of Canadians will result in not 187 railcars of hay moving West, but 711 railcars and more than 100 trucks of donated hay going from Central and Eastern Canada to Alberta and Saskatchewan. Using the donations of hay, equipment, fuel, inputs and funds received to date, more than 30,000 tonnes of donated hay will be provided to Western producers who need it. If the weather holds and donations continue to be received, more of that pledged hay will move. While we recognize that we are not going to be able to provide feed to every Western producer who needs it, the many letters and calls we have received from the West tell us that Hay West is making a difference. In fact, we encourage you to complete your work on this file by contacting producers and their organizations in Western Canada to ask them for their opinion of the Hay West Initiative.

Third fact: Contrary to the impression left by your article, the federal government's contribution to this project is modest. In fact, the government has only covered the costs of about half of the railcars used to transport donated hay. Furthermore, the cost to government for the railcars that it did supply was more like $125 to $150 per tonne, not $280 per tonne as your article states. This includes the $25 per tonne cost of fumigation, which is required by federal regulation, and which is being paid for by the federal government.

Fourth fact: Your article claims that the government is seeking to make "something of a situation that was never there" and that the prairie provinces could have supplied their farmers with feed. Estimates in July from the government of Alberta were of a need for 650,000 tonnes of additional hay. Since the rains in September, and the receipt of some Hay West hay, that need has dropped to 350,000 tonnes, but the need is clearly still there and will not likely be addressed solely by Western feed.

Fifth fact: Ontario producers and Canadian citizens do not believe that they have "saved the day" as is stated in your article. Donations and pledges are still coming in. No one who has contributed to this project believes that they have solved all of the problems, nor do they believe the job is done. We do believe, however, that our project has done a lot to raise the profile of the serious situation in Western Canada. The continued offers of hay, services, equipment, time and money clearly demonstrate that fact, and as long as the weather cooperates and the donations keep coming in, hay will continue to move.

But, all facts aside, Hay West is about more than just hay—it's about being a Canadian and about the genuine desire of Canadians to reach out to other Canadians in their time of need. Time and time again, during ice storms, floods, and now during the drought, citizens of this country have come to the aid of fellow Canadians. We are proud of this project and of the spirit of sharing that has come through, and we will continue to do our very best to help while there is still a need.

–Pierre Brodeur
General Manager
Hay West

Another "economics" story was found in an October 8, 2002, commentary published in the *Calgary Herald*. Danny Leroy, Assistant Professor at the University of Lethbridge, argued that it would have been better to give money spent on Hay West directly to affected farmers so that they could access feed by the most economical means available. The point he made was that it was unlikely that farmers, left to their own devices, would have bought hay from farmers some 4,000 kilometers away. Leroy's biggest beef was with subsidies and government intervention in the marketplace. "Farmers who make the wise decision to maintain hay reserves in the event of a drought must continue to compete with farmers who did not," he argued. "If it were not for the government intervention, imprudent farmers would go bankrupt and their farms taken over by more skilled and/or cautious farmers."[4]

While the portion of news coverage that focused on the economics of Hay West was very small, articles that drew the conclusion that Hay West was uneconomic did so without having examined all the facts and issues. In this regard, both Professor LeRoy's and Senator Sparrow's economic analyses are far from complete. They did not take into account that the hay was donated, not purchased. Farmers contributed every bale of hay that went west. Most farmers also cut, raked, baled and delivered the hay to the rail yard, the only exceptions being those who received some compensation through a donation made by the Government of Alberta. Second, the rail capacity that was used might well have been idle. A more relevant analysis might have been to examine purely incremental costs of Hay West operations. Third, the benefits of raising the profile of the plight of farmers suffering not just from the worst drought in 133 years, but a drought that had been building for three years, was not evaluated. Finally, what value would the professor give to the psychological lift given to Western farmers that had been steadily losing hope as the drought progressed? Some farmers might well have been encouraged to hold on and not sell their herds at depressed prices.

As for the numbers, the estimated value of the nearly 60,000 large bales of hay shipped was in excess of $6 million. Of course, the estimate is difficult to pin down since the price per bale of hay fluctuated wildly in Alberta and Saskatchewan over the summer of 2002. In fact, it was reported in some areas that hay fetched as much as $200 per bale, an amount that would double the estimated value of the shipments noted above.

Hay West spent about $1.1 million (net of the $200,000 surplus that was given to Western farmers); the government of Canada spent about $3.8 million on fumigation and rail transport; and other rail shipments not donated by CN and CP were valued at about $745,000. These expenses total about $5.4 million, $600,000 less than the estimated value of the hay. Contrary to what a few economists and politicians were saying, the numbers do not seem too far out of line. Of course, if you include the value of the time given by Eastern farmers to the cause, the whole project might not have been economical. But then again, how do you value a labor of love?

Another potential economic impact of Hay West—that of increasing the supply and thereby reducing the price for hay in the West—was not readily measurable. It was reported to Hay West that some Southern Alberta farmers had complained that large shipments of donated hay had impacted on the natural laws of supply and demand. Their problem was that as the year progressed the price of hay was going down. The year before, when Southern Alberta was in a drought, the price of hay rose to the benefit of Northern Alberta farmers. In 2002, Southerners thought they should now benefit because their crop was good. The Hay West organization did not enter the supply and demand debate but happily mused that if the price of hay was going down it was that much more affordable for those who couldn't grow enough on their farms to meet their needs.

The price of hay also made the news when accusations of price gouging for scarce Western hay were made. Alberta Premier Ralph Klein spoke out against the practice and asked all farmers to be reasonable and considerate. "This is terrible. It's now to be neighborly and fair and understand with compassion the plight of those farmers who are indeed suffering," said Klein.[5] One newspaper columnist was driven to wondering if the Alberta premier, ever the promoter of free market capitalism, was becoming a socialist. "The bitter irony for Alberta farmers is that the kindness of strangers is greater than neighbors. Farmers in Central and Eastern Canada are giving away hay to drought-stricken farmers. Now, that's neighborly. The image of warm-hearted Easterners takes a little getting used to. The feeling toward Central Canada has been frosty in the past. Especially when the government of Canada tried to institute the National Energy Program in 1980. . . . I want to hear Ralph Klein take the next step in his conversion and say, 'I think now is the time, not only to be neighborly but to remember that energy is the lifeblood of all Canada, and that pricing of our own energy is not the compassionate thing to do but the responsible thing to do.'"[6]

The most important number for Hay West was what ultimately got delivered to farms in Western Canada: 30,000 tonnes of hay. By any measure, that's a lot of hay. Laid end to end, the nearly 60,000 bales would stretch over 90 kilometers. It takes one ton of hay to feed a cow for a season. That means 30,000 head of cattle were fed as a result of the Hay West Initiative. And all this was accomplished in a few short months from a standing start in mid-July.

While the few who ventured views on the economics of Hay West were generally critical, their assessments turned out to be a relatively small part of the Hay West story, with their numbers being easily overwhelmed by the goodwill generated by generous farmers and other Canadians.

NOTES

1 Lorge, Ryan. "Sending Hay to Sask. a hoax." *Star-Phoenix* 25 August 2002, sec, A: 7. (The story was also reported by Roy McGregor in the *Globe and Mail* on 7 October 2002 under the title "Ottawa made hay out of bailout: Senator.")

2 Ibid.

3 Ibid.

4 LeRoy, Danny. "Hazy logic: Had farmers been given the cash wasted on shipping hay from the East, they'd be better off, this Lethbridge academic argues." *Calgary Herald* 8 October 2002, sec. A: 19

5 *Calgary Herald* News Services. "Klein says farmers gouged: Encourages hay producers in the south to be 'fair'." *Calgary Herald* 8 August 2002, sec. A: 5

6 Charbonneau, David. "Drought-stricken farmers have Klein thinking like a socialist." *Kamloops Daily News* 20 August 2002, sec. A: 6.

Public Recognition and Appreciation

Public fascination with Hay West was fueled by a phenomenal amount of press coverage. The attention was of such magnitude that Hay West now enjoys a place in Canadian history. Even before its place in the history books is confirmed, Hay West is showing up in popular culture in Canadian crossword puzzles and trivia board games.

Hay West was mentioned in over 1,600 newspaper, radio and television reports. In one prominent ranking of the top ten news stories of 2002, Hay West came in at number nine. *National Post* columnist Don Martin summarized Hay West with these words: "Ontario farmers send hay to drought-ravaged Western cattle producers. The cost of transporting the feed didn't make economic sense, but proved there's still a poignant East–West Canada connection in a nation dominated by North–South trade."[1]

Songs also paid tribute to Hay West. These include the tune "Make it Rain" by Terilyn Spooner and "Pass it On— A Song of Hope" by John Gracie, Helen Walk-Bowmen and Mike Lounibus, which became the Hay West anthem. Other tributes recalled the initiative in verse, like the poem "Here Comes the Hay" by Iverna Peplinski, which appeared in the *Renfrew Weekend News* on September 20, 2002:

> *Here comes the hay*
> *The Western farmer said*
> *It's coming from Ontario*
> *My cattle will be fed*

They are so happy
But it works both ways
For they helped us out
When the Ice Storm had its days
Now our farmers are wonderful
Their idea was great
As they shared out their hay
It was sent out by freight
It's a great way of sharing
When rain doesn't come
The ground dries all up
From the hot blazing sun
So hurray for the farmers
To help one another
It shows some good on earth
To share with each other.

Volunteers proudly wore their hats on Hay West Day at the Ottawa Renegades football game.
Photo: Hay West volunteer.

While Hay West was operational, the Ottawa Renegades of the Canadian Football League and Ottawa Mayor Bob Chiarelli declared September 22, 2002, as Hay West Day in Ottawa. In an effort led by Ottawa Councillor Doug Thompson, thousands of dollars were raised from ticket sales and cash donation boxes outside a football game against the Calgary Stampeders. Hay West was also recognized in a pre-game ceremony.

The biggest events held in support of Western farmers were the Say Hay concerts held at the Edmonton Coliseum and the Calgary Saddledome on the nights of October 12 and 13, 2002. Organized by Greg Thomas of Key Entertainment Group and produced by Canadian recording artist and Order of Canada member Tom Jackson, each concert featured close to fifty artists, including Jann Arden, George Fox, Paul Brandt, Doc Walk, Lisa Brokop, and

Michelle Wright, among many others. While Say Hay was not directly part of the Hay West Initiative, there was some obvious inspiration that went both ways.

Wyatt and Willard McWilliams were invited to attend the concerts and were graciously hosted in Calgary by Alberta Premier Ralph Klein. In his brief remarks at the concert, Premier Klein asked the crowd to acknowledge the McWilliams as the two people who started the relief movement. Could the McWilliams have possibly imagined such a scene three months earlier? Here they were receiving a standing ovation from thousands of Albertans.

The money raised by the concerts was used to create the Say Hay Assistance Program. In addition to sale of tickets, funds were raised through a silent auction, radio pledges and a national telethon. CBC *Newsworld* broadcast the Calgary concert live for national television. With the Say Hay money, as well as residual funds from Hay West given to Alberta 4-H, between $1,000 and $1,750 were given to approximately 800 farmers who had demonstrated substantial need. A similar program in

An ensemble cast of perform-
ers on stage for the Say Hay
benefit concert in Edmonton,
Alberta.
Photo: Cheryl McWilliams.

Saskatchewan helped farmers offset the cost of transporting hay within the province.

On December 18, 2002, the business in the City of
Ottawa Council Chambers was set aside for a reception
and presentation of the Key to the City to Wyatt and
Willard McWilliams. In his remarks, Mayor Bob
Chiarelli noted: "Unfortunately, for our Western farmers,
a three-year drought and an invasion of grasshoppers
forced many producers into near-bankruptcy this past
summer. There was no hope. That is until Wyatt and
Willard McWilliams started the Hay West campaign
from a kitchen table in Navan . . . . Next month, it will
be five years since our city and region suffered through
the Ice Storm of the century. Our Western neighbors
were there for us during our time of need. It was our turn
to say thank you through Hay West."

Willard, Wyatt and Cheryl
McWilliams at the podium
being saluted by Albertans at
the Say Hay concert in
Edmonton.
Photo: Hay West volunteer.

In accepting the Key to the City, Wyatt told City
Council how difficult and rewarding it was to be a farmer
in the year 2002. Wyatt also remarked that were times that

he visited the West when he might have been hesitant to tell his hosts he was from Ottawa. Now, he said, "When someone from Ottawa goes to Alberta and Saskatchewan, they may get a better welcome."

Willard used the occasion to speak of the generosity of so many Canadians. He then announced that the Hay West surplus of $200,000 was being donated to Alberta and Saskatchewan 4-H and other farm relief support groups to continue the drought relief effort.

Many farming groups and other organizations saluted Hay West and the McWilliams. Those honors included the Commemorative Medal for the Golden Jubilee of Her Majesty Queen Elizabeth II presented by MP Don Boudria.

The Annual Alberta Farm Classic Awards presented a special award to the McWilliams in Leduc, Alberta. Wyatt McWilliams was recognized as the Citizen of the Year in the *Eastender*, an on-line news publication in the Ottawa region. The Eastern Valley and Ottawa–Rideau Region Soil and Crop Improvement associations gave a plaque to the McWilliams. On presenting it, Jim Wallbridge said, "They brought big awareness that there was really a need for farming in this country. Our membership felt this is something that should be recognized."

In the fall of 2003, the McWilliams received the Meritorious Service Award from the Governor General of Canada. The award is given to people who made an

His Worship Bob Chiarelli
Mayor of the City of Ottawa
requests the pleasure of your company
at a Reception followed by a
Presentation of the "Key to the City"
in honour of
Willard McWilliams and
Wyatt McWilliams
Wednesday, December 18, 2002
12:00 p.m.
Ottawa City Hall
Jean Pigott Place and
Andrew Haydon Hall
110 Laurier Avenue West, Ottawa

R.S.V.P. (613) 580-2424 ext. 21245

Son honneur Bob Chiarelli
maire de la ville d'Ottawa
est heureux de vous inviter
à une réception suivie d'une cérémonie
de remise de la « clé de la Ville »
en l'honneur de
Willard McWilliams et de
Wyatt McWilliams
le mercredi 18 décembre 2002
à 12 h
hôtel de ville d'Ottawa
place Jean-Pigott et
salle Andrew-Haydon
110, avenue Laurier Ouest, Ottawa

R.S.V.P. (613) 580-2424 poste 21245

An invitation to attend the awarding of the Key to the City to Wyatt and Willard McWilliams.

outstanding contribution to Canadian society, at home and abroad, through their determination, talent and excellence.

Upon receiving this and every other award the McWilliams were quick to say that it was not they but the Hay West Initiative that was being recognized. In their view, all awards were to be shared by the thousands of farm-ers and other Canadians who gave of themselves to help fellow Canadians.

NOTES

1 Martin, Don. "I am not losing control." *National Post* 28 December 2002, Sec. RB: 2.

Lessons Learned

While Hay West may have looked impromptu at times, with 1,600 volunteers and success in moving close to 60,000 hay bales across the country, there is much that can be earned from this national relief effort.
Photo: Hay West volunteer.

Policy makers in government, lobbyists for the agriculture industry, or those who might desire to initiate a relief effort of their own would be wise to consider what can be learned from Hay West. Those who were close to the project identified the following 10 elements as critical to their success.

1.   Simple ideas—big dreams

It did not take a brilliant idea or an innovative process to launch Hay West. In fact, the whole concept was rather simple: respond to the shortage of hay in the West with the surplus from the East. The idea was easy to explain and grand enough to draw attention. While the McWilliams had no idea that Hay West would grow into what it did, they always believed that a massive relief effort was possible.

2.   Leadership

Every good idea or noble cause needs someone to go beyond identifying a problem. That means replacing the word *should* with *will*. In the case of Hay West, Willard and Wyatt McWilliams had not only the idea but also the courage to take the next step to reach out and ask for help. Leaders can't do the work by themselves, and the McWilliams were not shy about enlisting others for support.

3.   Persistence

There were many times when the Hay West organizers could easily have given up. Many things went wrong and many issues lingered. The McWilliams must have wondered what they had gotten themselves into when they were trucking hay to Brockville in mid-July. The fumigation issue was devastating in the short term, but they overcame the hurdle. Similarly, they were loading hay before they had an inkling of how it was going to be allocated and distributed out West, but knowing that what they were doing was at least possible, they tackled each obstacle as it arose and never considered giving up.

4. Clear mandate

In the midst of Hay West, it would have been easy for the organization to get involved in a wide variety of other activities to help Western farmers. There were certainly temptations to do just that, yet the organization stayed focused on the job they started: getting hay from the East to the West.

5. Good governance

Within one month of the relief effort first being conceived, Hay West had been incorporated with a board of directors. In hindsight, that was not fast enough.

The process of establishing a governance regime forces any well-meaning organization to understand who they are, what they are doing and how decisions must be made.

6. Financial systems

Hay West knew where it stood financially on a daily basis. To keep the initiative going and growing, organizers had to know the weakest link in the distribution chain so they could ask the most likely donor for help immediately.

7. Frugality

Hay West had a character that was attractive to Canadians. Those directly involved were caring, compassionate and modest people who sought no personal gain or recognition. No one was profiting from Hay West.

The goodwill around Hay West could have easily evaporated if money had been wasted or spent recklessly. Even a hint of lavish spending could have changed the perception of Hay West overnight.

8. Prudence in partnerships

In a volunteer, community-driven initiative, offers of support are rarely refused. But sometimes help comes with expectations and strings attached. Hay West learned that it would have been better to do more up-front due diligence with its prospective partners before entering into agreements. Dealing with people and groups of like mind and interest is a lot more enjoyable and productive.

9. Media relations

As the organizers commented on many occasions, media made Hay West. Without the daily broadcasts of progress and need, there is no way that Hay West would have attracted anywhere near the level of donations of hay from farmers and money from the corporate and private sectors. However noble the cause, unless people hear about it, not much will happen.

10. Government relations

In this era of partnerships, it's unrealistic to expect that governments will solve all the nation's problems. They may want to be helpful, but they are slow moving, bureaucratic and risk averse. Hay West demonstrated that government will help a good cause if the community and media take a substantial interest.

The Legacy—
Nation Building

The Canadian flag frequently adorned rail cars and trucks moving hay out West to show that Canadians care about one another.
Photo: Hay West volunteer.

It is one thing to deliver hay to drought-stricken farmers. It is quite another to be a positive force helping to draw a country together. It is clear from the commentary that Hay West was about far more than feeding animals—it was about strengthening a nation.

In a press interview, Wyatt McWilliams spoke about the many people who were affected by the drought and the relief effort. "It's bigger than anybody thought. I never dreamed of so much support or thought there was so much Canadian spirit and goodwill out there. Farmers are only 1 percent of the population, so we all have to pull together to support one another. But this drought is about more than hay—it's about communities, it's about people's livelihoods, it's about the future of car dealerships and machinery deal-

erships. Whole communities that depend on agriculture are on the brink of disaster in Western Canada."[1]

The editorial in Alberta's *Wainwright Review* of August 20, 2002, mused that the East wasn't the foe that the West had experienced of late. "Like everyone has been saying, it's great to see Eastern farmers helping out Western, and I'm sure if the tables were turned, the West would help the East. Canadian helping Canadian. It shows that we're all in this together, and that maybe farmers are farmers, regardless if they drive their tractors on this side of the Great Lakes or not."[2]

The same sentiments were echoed by people from across the country. Cattle and horse rancher Pat Allard from Chapleau, Quebec, said, "*Hay West* is a grassroots effort and goes to show that all the East–West stuff is about politics, not people."[3] Thousands of miles away in Rolly View, Alberta, Hay West lottery winner Bo Arvedson commented, "You can sure tell that the country has united more than ever. I think everyone has been positively affected by [Hay West]."[4]

Perhaps nowhere did Hay West's gesture toward nation-building have more impact that among members of Kevin Sorenson's constituency association in Camrose, Alberta, one the areas hardest hit by the drought. Before Hay West, many did not speak favorably of anything coming from the East—in fact they were often the voice of Western alienation. When they thought about what Hay West meant to them, they came up with the idea for a hat. The words on the hat were about far more than hay. They read: "Thanks Hay West—Canada United."

Because of Hay West, MP Kevin Sorenson was not shy about talking about national unity in his home province. As the trains began to arrive with donated Eastern hay in Wainwright, Sorenson remarked, "Welcome to a country where people care about people, where farmers care about farmers, a country that is united in its time of need. This is a great day for Canada."[5]

Ottawa Citizen reporter Peter Zimonjic, who followed the Hay West story, seemed to agree with this sentiment and attached this observation at the end of his front page story of August 6, 2002: "But if there is one thing for certain in all this, it is that this experience has brought this country closer together. The gesture of kindness by Eastern Ontario farmers will go a lot farther than the hay will, and it will be remembered for a great many years to come."[6]

Long after the drought of 2002, the Hay West story continued to inspire acts of nation-building. In December 2003, CBC *Newsworld* covered the efforts of two Newfoundland girls trying to save starving Alberta horses that were also victims of the 2002 drought. Calling the new cause "Nay West," CBC's Susan Peddler told the story: "When the two girls saw a newspaper headline that read 'Desperate Alberta rangers forced to kill horses,' they decided to do something. So they launched a website, www.savealbertahorses.com, to highlight the problem. Alberta's horses are in trouble because last summer's drought on the prairies means not enough feed."[7]

The example of generosity shown by Hay West was on the mind of Joe Niessen of Carstairs, Alberta, when, in 2003, forest fires ravaged the interior of British Columbia. Niessen, a Hay West recipient, was reported as saying, "It's our turn to help," as he and other Alberta farmers, under the leadership of Ben Penner, trucked hay to needy B.C. farmers. When trucking regulations held up the trucks at Golden, B.C., the local hospitality industry and residents

A hat from Kevin Sorenson's Alberta riding association. Not long before Hay West, many in this group might have considered themselves alienated Westerners. Photo: Bob Plamondon.

The children of Meadowview Public School singing the national anthem before the start of the closing ceremonies for Hay West on October 31, 2002.
Photo: Hay West volunteer.

came to the convoy's rescue, offering free hotel, meals and whatever equipment and manpower was necessary to get the trucks back on the road. "The people of Golden heard about it and got really incensed over it," said Penner. "The mayor was out, the Member of the Legislative Assembly was out, and they all helped our drivers. That was great."[8]

At the closing ceremonies for Hay West at Wyatt McWilliams' farm on October 31, 2002, about 100 friends,

family and donors reflected upon what had been accomplished over the previous three months. "We all got to see, firsthand, what it means to be a Canadian," said Wyatt. "Time and time again, during ice storms, floods, and now during the drought, citizens of the country have come to the aid of fellow Canadians. We are proud of this project and of the spirit of sharing that has come through." Fittingly, the ceremony began with a rendition of "Oh

Canada," sung by the children of Meadowview Public School from Navan, Ontario. The children obviously enjoyed their roles for the day, especially the opportunity to inscribe messages of friendship on the wrapped bales of the last shipment that headed West. Somehow it seemed fitting that the last words to be written about Hay West and what it meant to those involved should come from the next generation of Canadians. Watching them happily writing their notes gave their parents hope that they could grow up to be farmers—farmers who will carry on the tradition of neighbor helping neighbor that has always distinguished the lives of those who make their living on the land.

Whatever endures from Hay West, it can be certain that Canada will have been made better for it. Better for unleashing a spirit of generosity that helps people in need, better for having brought the nation together in ways that might not have predicted and better for showing that those without inherent power and influence can make a difference. It makes you think that if Hay West was possible, then everything is possible.

NOTES

1 Zimonjic, Peter "A Eastern farmer by trade, a hero out West by action." *Ottawa Citizen* 18 August 2002, sec. A: 4

2 Clemmer, Kelly "No Longer East vs. West". *Wainwright Review* 20 August 2002, sec. A: 4.

3 Zimonjic, Peter "A Eastern farmer by trade, a hero out West by action." *Ottawa Citizen* 18 August 2002, sec. A: 4.

4 Ibid.

5 Zimonjic, Peter. "'I won't have to sell my herd': Western farmers praise generosity of Ontario brethren." *Ottawa Citizen* 6 August 2002, sec. A: 1.

6 Ibid.

7 *Aid*. CBC-TV, Toronto. 7 December 2002

8 Williamson, Kerry. "Hay wagon train hits rut in B.C.: Feed donation caravan held up by bureaucrats." *Calgary Herald* 1 November 2003, Sec. A: 10.

Appendices

The following corporations made generous donations of cash and kind to Hay West:

Addison Energy • Alberta Agriculture Food and Rural Development • ARC Resources Ltd. • Atlas Energy • Bank of Nova Scotia • Bonterra Energy Corporation • Canadian Association of Petroleum Producers • Canadian Mortgage and Housing Corporation • Canadian Pacific Rail • CDI Education • Chevron • Canada Resources • CN Rail • CP Rail • Devon Canada Corp • Dominion Energy Canada Ltd. • Enerplus Global Energy Management Company • Farm Credit Canada • First Energy Capital Corp • Fortune Energy Inc. • Husky Energy • Imperial Oil • John Deere • Kelsey's and Montana Restaurants • Key Entertainment Group • Mancal Energy Inc. • Molson Canada • Nexen Canada Ltd. • Norampac Inc. • Northrock Resources • Oiltech Resources Ltd. • Olympia Energy Inc. • Ottawa Central Railway • Petro-Canada • Pfizer • Power Corporation of Canada • PrimeWest Management Inc. • Progressive Conservative Party of Canada • Provident Energy Ltd. • Royal Canadian Mint • Samson Canada Ltd. • Shell Oil, Calgary • Southward Energy Ltd. • Sundre Petroleum Operations Group • Synapticmedia • Syncor • Terraquest Energy Corporation • UPI Inc., Ontario • Upton Resources Inc.

While the Hay West Initiative eventually received the assistance of over 1,600 volunteers, the following deserve special recognition for having served as community coordinators of the relief effort:

ONTARIO

Barwick/Rainy River
   Kim Bliss
Belleville
   George McNeely, Cindy Hubble and George Hiemlaw
Brockville
   Wyatt McWilliams, Marjorie and Mike Wencoff
Cobourg
   John Boughen, Tom Barrie and Jim Tunney
Havelock
   Scott Stewart and Norm Blodgett
Kingston
   George Sutherland, Dudley Shannon, Jason Pike and John Williams
Ottawa
   Marjorie and Mike Wencoff, John Hickling and Wyatt McWilliams
Pembroke
   Donna Campbell, Stewart Hamel and Eve Yantha
Sault Ste. Marie
   Dale Laroe, Barb Wallace and "GP Flake Board"
Shakespeare
   Martin Ritsma, Carl Richson and Murray Pfiefer
Smiths Falls
   Charlene Renkema, Eleanor Renaud, Cathy Willoughby and Wyatt McWilliams
Snelgrove
   Allan Thompson, Beth Laidlaw, John Lyons and David Armstrong

Welland
   Gerry Winnicki
Utopia/Barrie
   Robert Ange and Larry Millar
Verner
   Darlene Bowen

QUEBEC

Bristol
   Jack Graham
Bromont/Foster
   Donna Donaldson, Milda Weiss, Aime Jacob and Max Auckstuhl
Lachute
   Ian Brass and Storrs McCaul
Valleyfield/Coteau Landing
   Tom Quinnell, Richard Belleveau and Harold Morson

NEW BRUNSWICK

Campbellton
   Weibe Dykstra and Don Gilbert
Moncton
   Wiebe Dykstra

NOVA SCOTIA

Amherst
   Donna Langill and Doug Bacon
Truro
   Donna Langill and Doug Bacon
Windsor
   Donna Langill and Doug Bacon

Hay West—By the Numbers

PLEDGES

Ontario	73,029
Quebec	15,629
PEI	1,553
New Brunswick	12,377
Nova Scotia	6,875
	109,463

SHIPMENTS

Rail cars	711
Trucks	161
Hay bales	57,918
Tonnes	30,000

RAIL CAR DONATIONS

Government of Canada	376
CN	97
CP	90
Say Hay	75
First Energy	50
Molson	20
Trans Canada Pipelines	2
PC Party Caucus	1
	711

LOTTERY

Alberta participants	3,500
Saskatchewan participants	5,000
Lottery winners	1,400

OTHER FACTS

It takes one ton of hay to feed a cow for a season. That means 30,000 head of cattle were fed as a result of Hay West.

A large round bale of hay weighs about 1,800 pounds with dimensions of approximately 5 feet high and 4 feet wide.

A large square bale measures approximately 8 feet by 3 feet and weighs 1,000 pounds.

A large round bale of hay is the equivalent of 18 small square bales. That means that Hay West shipped the equivalent of over one million small square bales.

Stacked on top of one another, 60,000 large bales would stretch 56.8 miles. That's the CN Tower times 165.